# WALES IS CLOSED

# Wales is Closed

## The quiet privatisation of British Steel

**Ralph Fevre**

SPOKESMAN

First published in 1989 by:
Spokesman
Bertrand Russell House
Gamble Street
Nottingham, England
Tel. 0602 708318

**British Library Cataloguing in Publication Data**
Fevre, Ralph
Wales is closed
    1. Wales
    I. Title
    338.4'7669142'09429

ISBN 0-85124-466-1
ISBN 0-85124-476-9 pbk

Printed by the Russell Press Ltd, Nottingham
(Tel. 0602 784505)

# Contents

**For Maureen and Natasha**

# Preface and Acknowledgments

I went to Port Talbot in 1982 to do what sociologists call a 'community study' of a town with high unemployment. As things turned out, I did a lot of things that someone doing a community study would do. I moved, reluctantly, to Port Talbot. It is hardly the prettiest of towns and I had lived for three months in the pleasant western suburbs of Swansea, but moving there was one of my conditions of employment and so for a year I lived in a £60-per-month flat next to the railway line in the centre of town. For the remaining twenty months of my contract I lived rather more comfortably in a bungalow in one of the 'better' parts of town — a ward that regularly returns a ratepayer candidate at local elections.

I took part in the social life of Port Talbot, I talked to lots of people and I joined the local Labour Party. These are all things which might be considered necessary for a community study. But this sort of study is usually thought of as a bit of unusual *anthropology*: unusual because you are doing it in your own society and not in Papua-New Guinea or amongst the Inuit. The familiarity means that you have to be especially on your guard against 'going native'. You are not supposed to lose your sense of being an outsider and begin to identify with the people you are 'studying'. I did.

For three years Port Talbot was my town as well, and I hope the people who live in Port Talbot will grant me the right to talk about them and their town as *more* than an outsider. Like many of them, I went there to work: they were drawn to Port Talbot by the work which was created when the steelworks were built in the town. I went there because of the unemployment that was created when massive redundancies were announced in the steelworks. This book is about how that unemployment was created *and recreated* and how it affected the lives of many people in the town. In particular it records the way in which permanent jobs were replaced by temporary jobs which condemned sections of the population to frequent spells of unemployment.

The research on which the book is based was funded by the Economic and Social Research Council (grant GOO 230048/1). Throughout the research I received considerable help and encouragement from the 'Steel Project' team at University College of Swansea and from other colleagues there: Chris Harris, Ray M. Lee, Lydia Morris, Griselda Leaver, Bill Bytheway, Phil Brown and Ethne Jeffreys. Ethne Jeffreys also typed the first draft of this book (provisionally titled 'How Many People Work At BSC?') for which, as with many other things, my heartfelt thanks. Later drafts were typed by Pat Ormond and Carol Cook. Carol Cook produced the final typescript with some help from the author (for which indirect thanks are due to Mike Whitaker for providing the hardware).

I would also like to thank the organisations and individuals I consulted during my fieldwork: the Iron and Steel Trades Confederation (especially the research department), BSC Port Talbot, West Glamorgan County Council Central Research Unit, the staffs of Port Talbot Job Centre and MSC Wales, and the people of Port Talbot (especially Brendan). Where they appear in the book I have given these people — and some firms — fictional names, and have altered other less significant details in order to preserve the confidentiality of those men and women who were kind enough to agree to be interviewed. The list of interviewees included BSC employees, trade union officers and officials, BSC managers, managers in contracting firms, representatives of employers' organisations and the employees of contracting firms. In addition, two hundred and ninety four residents of Port Talbot took part in the survey reported in Chapter Six, for which my thanks (thanks which are also due to Margaret and her colleagues for their work on the interviews for this survey).

Ralph Fevre
University College of North Wales
Bangor, Gwynedd

# Chapter One

# The Quiet Privatisation of British Steel

On 10th July 1983 the Industry Secretary told the House of Commons of his intention to denationalise all of those industries reporting to him during the life of that parliament. In effect, he was merely repeating the Government's earlier statement of its intentions when entering office in 1979, but the nationalised steel industry was not sold into private hands until November *1988*. The Government's failure to sell the British Steel Corporation (BSC) to the private sector over nine years requires some explanation, especially in view of the Government's apparent determination to overcome all manner of obstacles where privatisation is concerned. In the first place, the Government has shown itself willing to privatise utilities like gas and telecommunications even though many people believe that State ownership of these services avoids wasteful duplication of supply networks. The Government has solved this problem only by dispensing with its commitment to increase competition in the provision of goods and services. Duplication of networks has not yet occurred on a large scale because the Government has handed effective *monopolies* to the new private owners of these businesses. In the second place, the Government has continued to encourage privatisation even when it is shown, as in the National Health Service, that this leads to deterioration in services and may well cost the nation more in the long run.[1] Finally, privatisation has continued even when common sense has dictated that the time was not right for further sales and that shares might fetch higher prices on another occasion. Indeed, the BSC sale was itself considered to be a 'rush job' by at least one commentator. BSC was sold as soon as it had showed a profit for three consecutive years — thought to be the City's *minimum* requirement for a successful flotation (*Guardian*, 25 November 1987). It seems that nothing has deterred the Government in its headlong rush to sell off all the nationalised companies regardless of the costs or consequences of these sales; but why should a government which is so wholeheartedly committed to privatisation have delayed the sale of one of the most important nationalised industries, steel? The short answer is: *up to 1988, nobody wanted to buy it.*

The delay occurred because it took the Government nine years to turn BSC into a profitable company: whereas other nationalised industries moved into the black in the countdown to privatisation, BSC's accounts showed losses year after year. BSC did not rise out of the red until the financial year 1985/6 when it showed a small profit for the first time in a decade. Clearly, the difficulties of making BSC a profitable concern are tremendous. UK steel is produced in circumstances which do little to encourage private investors.[2]

In particular, the product market is much less buoyant than on the last occasion steel was denationalised in 1953 (the most recent nationalisation of steel took place in 1967 but there was a brief period of state control between 1950 and 1953). Home demand for steel in 1987 was still one quarter below 1979 levels. Exports had increased but this improvement may have been due to favourable exchange rates (*Guardian*, 9 December 1987) and the problems of world output and demand remained. The trade unions have repeatedly argued that BSC reduced output *in advance* of falling demand, that is, that BSC management exacerbated the consequences of a 'world glut' of steel for the UK industry. Nevertheless, there is still substantial excess capacity in basic steelmaking throughout Europe, despite the EEC's efforts to co-ordinate a reduction in output. The EEC's steel workforce dropped from 796,000 to 480,000 between 1974 and 1983, but another 100,000 jobs were scheduled to disappear before 'reconstruction' was completed. Furthermore, the EEC predicted that demand for steel would continue to decline in the 1980s and that the decline would become even more rapid in the 1990s. (*Guardian*, 8 July 1985). Competition from steel producers *outside* Europe has also increased. The latest figures show, for example, that the volume of steel produced in the UK is now only slightly greater than that produced in South Korea (*ESRC Newsletter*, March 1985). Stiff international competition, together with EEC regulation of capacity, means that a privatised BSC will not find it easy to increase its market share and therefore improve profits through increased sales.

The Government tried to stop pouring money into BSC simply in order to allow the industry to stand still. Since first entering office in 1979, successive Conservative administrations attempted to force BSC to achieve a 'break-even' point where investment became self-financing and losses would not be underwritten by the Government. The trade unions always argued that this was premature and they were proved right each year when the Government were forced to re-schedule the 'break-even' target date.

The cost of BSC's small operating profit in 1985/6 was hidden in the £2,530m of losses (£869m in 1982/3 alone) made over the previous five years of rationalisation. Much of this money was spent in reducing the size of BSC's workforce in order to achieve profitability. When the Conservative Government took over in 1979 BSC employed 186,000 people (Morgan, 1983). Five years later employment at BSC had been reduced by nearly sixty per cent to just under 79,000, (*Observer*, 5 August 1984). By the time BSC moved into profit a total of 132,000 jobs had been lost, (*Guardian*, 17 July 1986). When BSC was eventually sold at 'prices the private sector can afford' (as promised in 1979), the total cost of privatisation amounted to £7 billion of losses in earlier years and a forty per cent mark-down of BSC's assets for the sale (*Guardian*, 5 December 1987). But such figures do not disclose the *manner* in which BSC was brought to profitability and hence to the market. In particular, they hide the fact that a substantial proportion of the seventy-five per cent reduction in BSC employment by 1987 was achieved by moving jobs to the private sector *in advance* of the BSC flotation.

According to Kevin Morgan: 'for Thatcherism, the restructuring and partial privatisation of the nationalised steel industry undoubtedly constitutes one of its most successful accomplishments' (Morgan, 1983: 189). The transfer of jobs to the private sector was achieved in two ways: by selling off parts of BSC, and by bringing in contractors. The former began with the sale of 'peripheral' activities. BSC does, or *did*, many other things apart from the basic steelmaking discussed above, and few of these 'peripheral' activities are undertaken on the sites of the five integrated steel plants, (Port Talbot, Llanwern, Scunthorpe, Teesside and Ravenscraig). Most of them fall into one of two categories. They may still be concerned with producing steel but, if so, both the method of production and the product are *specialised*, as in the specialist steels of Sheffield for example. Alternatively, they may be concerned with a stage in production which is much nearer to the final consumer — for example, the manufacture of steel tubes or wire. This 'horizontal' and 'vertical' integration was in part created with (re)nationalisation in 1967, but also in BSC's subsequent expansion and diversification. Circumstances changed, however (a major cause of the change in circumstances was the 1981 Iron and Steel Bill, see Morgan, 1983: 180), and BSC was soon under instructions from the Government to set up private companies to run these 'peripheral' activities. This policy caused concern for the steel trade unions, including the largest of these unions, the Iron and Steel Trades Confederation (ISTC). In its evidence to the House of Commons Committee on Trade and Industry the ISTC noted that

'In its report three months ago, Inter Company Comparisons predicted that one fifth of British private steel firms could disappear in the near future ... But this is only one part of the story. Side by side with the collapse of the old private sector, there is emerging a new private sector fashioned out of the body of the British Steel Corporation. 1981 saw Allied Steel and Wire, 1982 brought Sheffield Forgemasters and 1983 has brought British Bright Bar. There may yet be a similar company formed in the special engineering steels sector and discussions are proceeding about cold rolled narrow strip. There is also a proposed scheme for rationalising the wiredrawing sector, and foundry rationalisation schemes are well advanced. Meanwhile, BSC has committed a number of its activities to free standing wholly owned subsidiaries and one of these — BSC (Chemicals) — has largely been sold to Bitmac Ltd., its former subsidiary. Earlier RDL was sold to Trafalgar House for £10 million.

'There is a great deal of public money involved in all these trans-actions, but the information divulged about them has been meagre and late.' (House of Commons Committee on Trade and Industry, 1983).

The ISTC thought, it seems, that denationalisation in steel had proceeded in some secrecy. At the least, it was (and is) a very *quiet* form of privatisation which provided a stark contrast to the hullabaloo which surrounded other sales of State-owned businesses. Yet privatisation, though quiet, was effective: by June 1984, 50 per cent of Allied Steel and Wire was owned by GKN; 50 per cent of Sheffield Forgemasters was owned by Johnson Firth Brown; and 40 per cent of British Bright Bar was owned by GKN while 20 per cent was owned by British Rolling Mills Ltd; Redpath Dorman Long (RDL) was wholly owned by Trafalgar House.[3] According to BSC's annual report for 1984/5 the book value of assets privatised or sold in the previous five years amounted to £349m (plus £74m of property sales).

In its 1984 Conference Report the ISTC claimed that

'The privatisation of the British Steel Corporation continues with the appointment of Mr Robert Haslam as Chairman of BSC. Mr Haslam has publicly acknowledged his commitment to create units of BSC that would be attractive to private capital and his acceptance of this aspect of Conservative Party policy within his terms of reference. However, there are some signs that he now sees the impracticability of pursuing such policies.

'Nonetheless BSC is ... being stripped of groups of mills which are then merged into private mills ... examples ... are Seamless Tube plc and Cold Drawn Tube plc ...'

Both this and the earlier (1983) statement from ISTC suggested that, even in the case of 'peripheral' activities, some difficulties remained in creating a profitable business which would prove attractive to the private sector. Thus GKN was reported to want £100m in return for its participation in a plan to extend its ownership of former BSC assets (*Observer*, 22 April 1984), and the 'quasi-private' Sheffield Forgemasters was soon in difficulty. Sheffield Forgemasters suffered losses and under-used capacity after its creation in 1982. BSC remained 'in the driving seat' and Forgemasters had to beg the Government for cash aid. Merchant bankers concluded that the Government had under-financed the venture when it was set up (*Guardian*, October 1984).

The ISTC statements also suggest that BSC management did not wholly agree with the policy (of privatisation) they were forced to pursue. Confirmation of both of these suggestions came in the reply given by the Chief Executive of BSC, Bob Scholey, at the ISTC's 1984 Conference, in answer to a question about extending privatisation to new areas:

> 'The present Government policy is to privatise, there can be no doubt about that ... Privatisation is not the easiest thing. You can't privatise without demonstrating profitability ... Nobody is going to put money into a plant or works which doesn't subscribe to these criteria ... The policy at the moment is in respect of fringe activities ... We try to set them up as Companies Act companies as soon as we can ... From the management point of view, we would be very hesitant to do it.'

Despite the difficulties of Sheffield Forgemasters those businesses which were sold had none of the drawbacks for private investors which were detailed (above) in the case of basic steelmaking. Compared to the large integrated steel plants, these businesses are small (therefore manageable for private owners) and require only modest levels of capital investment. In spite of the problems encountered in all the markets for steel products, they enjoy more buoyant demand. Where BSC *close* a plant and withdraw from a particular sector of the market, they leave the way open for new, private ventures which may, for example, produce on a smaller scale or in a different way. In this respect steel resembles coal: the closure of NCB pits in South Wales has been accompanied by an increase in the number of small, private drift mines (as well as in the number of, more widely publicised, opencast sites).[4]

Even senior BSC managers apparently believed that although it was not easy to sell off 'fringe activities', it was a damn sight harder to sell off basic steelmaking. Yet they might have had difficulty in describing some of the work undertaken by the new private firms in the industry as 'fringe activities'. Although the problems of finding a profitable unit to sell off were even more severe, there were signs that the Government would like to privatise elements of steel production which were neither specialised nor concerned with manufacturing processes close to the final consumer, but were undertaken *on the sites* of the large integrated steel plants. In its

evidence to the Trade and Industry Committee, ISTC noted that
the Government and BSC had made a commitment to continue
steel production, but

> 'The commitment is to *steelmaking* at the major sites. Lots of other
> things happen there however, so this statement leaves the way open
> either to closure (in order to remove BSC facilities competing with the
> private sector) or privatisation. The second possibility of privatisation
> seems more likely for it would be consistent with the intentions of the
> *Iron and Steel Act (1981)* to push BSC out of certain parts of the market.
> The model for the future might thus appear to be Scunthorpe works
> with heavy iron and steelmaking (public sector) cheek by jowl with
> rolling mills and finishing departments (modernised or installed at
> public expense but now privately owned). In short there will be a public/
> private division not within the product range but between production
> (public) and rolling and finishing (private).'

While the most profitable parts of BSC were being sold off, the
large integrated steel plants could hardly be called profitable. Given
the problems of creating a profitable unit even within BSC's
'peripheral' activities, there must have been some doubt as to
whether the Scunthorpe case *would* provide a model for the other
large plants. In fact BSC found an alternative means to achieve the
same end, one which did not involve persuading the private sector
to buy a part of these plants, or even to take up residence on these
sites. Privatisation in the integrated plants took the form of a
reduction in direct employment *and a parallel increase in the
proportion of work undertaken by private contractors*[5]. In other
words, BSC put out to contract some of the work previously done by
BSC employees. This, the second aspect of the quiet privatisation of
British Steel, provides the focus for the rest of this book. The
subject of this study is, however, unemployment.

*The Fitters' Stories.*
It is likely that the most substantial increase in the use of contractors
by BSC has been at its Port Talbot works. This book is concerned
with what happened at BSC Port Talbot between 1980 and 1985,
that is with how large numbers of the employees of *private* firms
came to work in one of Britain's *nationalised* steelworks. But the
book is not simply an account of changes in industrial organisation
and of the economic arguments behind these changes. It is also a
story about the people of Port Talbot, of how their lives have been
changed by 'economics'. One in five of a random sample of men in
Port Talbot (see Chapter Five) had worked for a contracting firm at
BSC at some time. The experience is obviously a common one:
what is it like and what are the consequences for the people
involved? The pages that follow describe the lives of some Port

Talbot residents at the point (in 1985) when I concluded my fieldwork.

'Frank Clark' is forty years old and works as a fitter. He lives with his wife, who works in an estate agent's office and a son who works in the Health Service. They own a video recorder, two cars and a motorbike, and Frank is a regular at one of the livelier local pubs. In the 1960s the term 'affluent worker' came to mean a manual worker who was not obviously hard up for money and could afford to purchase the more expensive consumer durables and a foreign holiday each year. Frank doesn't take holidays abroad but he is an 'affluent worker' in many respects, *except one*: in the six years from January 1979 he had eleven different jobs and eleven separate periods of unemployment.

The length of Frank's jobs varied from a maximum of two years to a minimum of two weeks. The length of his spells of unemployment varied from a couple of days to five months. (He had eight completed spells of more than a week.) In all eleven jobs Frank was employed as a fitter. Six of them were with the same firm but Frank also worked for five other firms over the five years. All of these firms were contractors and most of the jobs were on contracts at BSC Port Talbot. Although he has also worked on contracts at chemical plants and oil refineries, there is, in fact, only one part of the steelworks where Frank has *not* worked, and yet he has never been a BSC employee. Frank has never been dismissed and has never left a job voluntarily. All his jobs have ended when the contract, or at least his part of the work for that contract, was completed.

Before taking up contracting work, which Frank calls 'The Life', he was employed continuously for fifteen years with a private steelmaking firm. When this firm closed in 1978 Frank received £1,500 redundancy pay: £100 for each year of service. He found a place on a training course at the Skill Centre after redundancy and received a £38-per-week allowance while he trained in general fitting and maintenance. He left the course to go straight into a job with a contracting firm, and until the summer of 1983 he was fortunate in that his spells out of work never exceeded three months and were usually much shorter. But after a two-week stint on the July shutdown at BSC Port Talbot — a 'stop fortnight' in which BSC employees are on holiday and various parts of the works are turned over exclusively to repair and maintenance — he was unemployed until Christmas Eve. This 'affluent worker' had an uninterrupted spell of 145 days on unemployment benefit alone. This spell ended in ironic circumstances: he had no money to spend over Christmas but it hardly mattered in the end because he had to work over the holiday!

While out of work, Frank regularly visits all the contracting firms which have his name on their books. He is 'on the books' of the firm which gave him a job on Christmas Eve but has been unemployed twice since then. That job lasted through spring 1984 but Frank was out of work again come autumn. He started again in September, back at BSC with another contractor. Frank said this was a good job. He earned a basic £3.30 an hour and was the first local fitter to be taken on. He was also able to get some of his friends jobs with the same firm. In May 1985 Frank became unemployed again; the job had lasted eight months. He counts himself lucky, much luckier than some, but he knows that even when he has a job, he could be out of work tomorrow and facing another extended period on the dole

'Job security is virtually non-existent. They can't afford to keep you when work dries up.'

All in all, it's just as well Frank's wife and son are, for the present at least, in work. Frank would like to get out of contracting work altogether and into a job which offered some security. He would be prepared to do anything, and doesn't feel he would have to follow his trade. Despite all the redundancies at the steelworks, Frank thinks his best chance of a secure job would be with BSC itself but, realistically, knows he has little hope when he is competing for a handful of vacancies with ex-BSC workers and the sons of current BSC employees.

'Barry Kitchen' and his friend 'Wyndham Thomas' are ex-BSC workers. They were made redundant, along with thousands of others, in 1980. Like Frank they are both fitters. Wyn worked for BSC for sixteen years, mainly as a maintenance fitter. Barry worked for fifteen years as a fitter and turner in BSC's Central Engineering Shop. Wyn is fifty-five and married with two daughters — one just married, the other engaged. The next wedding, like the last, will be a 'good do' and, like Frank, Wyn has all the outward appearances of the 'affluent worker'. He was made compulsorily redundant, despite his desperate attempts to hang on, in July 1980. He received a 'lumper' of £11,000 redundancy money. This money came in useful in the following four months when Wyn was out of work. A spell at the Skill Centre was followed by another eight months of unemployment, then Wyn got his first job with a contracting firm at the steelworks, doing *exactly* the same work that he used to do when employed by BSC. But this contract came to an end and Wyn was unemployed again for several months before finding work, as a supervisor, with another firm which had a contract at the steelworks. From here he went straight into a job with a local engineering company which does some contract work for BSC on its own premises, but like Frank, he would dearly love to work for BSC (again). BSC have Wyn's name on file and he believes preference will be shown for people like himself, who suffered *compulsory* redundancy, if vacancies arise. He has heard of one bloke being taken back recently and Wyn is going to keep his ears open to make sure that those who were forced to accept redundancy are considered first.

Barry Kitchen could have played professional football. He had trials with teams in Bristol and the Midlands and signed forms for one of the big Birmingham clubs. But he got homesick and came back to Port Talbot, met his wife and soon had a young child to care for. He is now thirty-three and lives in a small terraced house with his wife, two children (with another on the way) and his widowed mother. He has a reputation as a militant trade-unionist, a voluble socialist and does a nice line in home brew. He took voluntary redundancy from BSC in May 1981 and received 'a nice lumper' in return. He was unemployed for a few weeks and then found a place on a welding course. The course lasted for twelve months and he received an allowance of £115 a week plus travelling expenses. When the course finished he was out of work for two weeks before he found work with a contracting firm back at BSC. To begin with he only got the odd shift here and there but in time the work became continuous. Most of it was at BSC but, unlike Wyndham Thomas — who he met while on this job — Barry was not doing the same work that he had done as a BSC employee. He was now doing *maintenance* fitting whereas his job for BSC had been on the lathes in the workshop. Barry was laid off at the same time as Wyn but found work again within a week. The job was as a fitter and welder with a contractor but off the BSC site. Here Barry was doing the same work as at BSC — this firm had taken on a lot of the jobs which BSC used to have performed in its own Central Engineering shop — as well as some welding (which he had learnt when retraining after redundancy). After a while a vacancy came up in this firm and Barry told Wyn to apply. For a while the two mates worked together; their respective gross earnings added up to £5,800 a year, that is more than £1,000 less than they had been earning five years before at BSC. Barry has now moved on to better things. He is a foreman with another contractor and, like Frank with *his* last firm, he has been able to arrange some jobs for his friends. It wouldn't surprise him if Wyn was soon on the move too.

'Richard Lewis' (Dick) used to work in BSC's Central Engineering Shop as a fitter, like Barry Kitchen. He trained as a fitter with the RAF and had twenty three years with BSC before taking voluntary redundancy at the age of fifty-seven in 1980. He used the 'lumper' of £12,000 to buy and improve the council house he lives in with his wife (all his children have grown up and moved away). Some of the money went on his hobby however. Dogs are Dick's passion: he breeds and shows spaniels and they now have very well-appointed kennels.

After redundancy Dick was unemployed for a while and then took up a place on a panel-beating course at the Skill Centre for which he received a £54-per-week allowance. In the two and a half years after the course ended Dick had spells of unemployment and spells of self-employment trying to use his new skill. Often he worked for less than £40 per week and after a spell of unemployment which lasted over Christmas 1983, he landed a job with a contractor at BSC. In the first instance the job only lasted three weeks but Dick's neighbour got a 'more permanent' job with the same firm and so, in time, did Dick. In fact Dick and the neighbour, Frederick, are only employed for five days at a time and don't know until the end of the week whether there will be work for them the following Monday. Nevertheless, they were still in the same job in the spring of 1985, labouring at the steelworks where they were once craftsmen — and earning £2.10 per hour. As Dick said, 'It's better than the dole.'

'Carl Roach' is twenty-four and six foot four inches tall. Until recently he played rugby for one of the less successful Welsh club sides, but has had to give up the game through injury. He has had two jobs since completing an apprenticeship as a diesel fitter. The first was for a firm which was contracted by BSC to provide internal transport around the steelworks. Carl worked on their fleet of lorries and earned £2.20 per hour. But the contract only lasted for twelve months and, when tenders went in for the new contract in 1981, Carl's firm was undercut. Except for a brief spell of employment with a local manufacturing firm, Carl has been unemployed ever since. He is married and has two young children. They live in a council house on the massive Sandfields housing estate. Fortunately, his wife has recently found a job as an insurance clerk. Carl now stays at home to look after the youngest child, except on Saturdays when he goes to watch the rugby team he used to play for and then his old team mates buy him a drink in the club after the match.

'Peter Smith's' wife doesn't work. They live, with a six-month-old daughter, in a damp rented flat in the most rundown area of Port Talbot. Peter has spent nearly half of his seven 'economically active' years since leaving school out of work. Like Frank, Carl and the rest, Peter is a skilled man, another fitter and turner. He did not finish his apprenticeship but took a six-month training course in 1980. In April 1983 he got a job labouring for a contractor at the steelworks. This job lasted for six months at £2 per hour. Peter was then laid off for two weeks. He got another two weeks' work in December but was laid off again on Christmas Eve (the day Frank Clark started work again). The job was supposed to begin again on 14th February but the start was delayed. In the last week of February Peter was 'expecting a phone call any time' but the call never came. The last he heard was that the foreman of the gang he worked with had himself given up waiting and had found a job in Cardiff. Peter is thinking about training again. He says computers are taking over but they will need people to repair them. All the mechanical courses are out of date but he'd like to do electronics, if only he could get a place on a course.

*Unemployment and 'Under-employment'.*
As the stories of each of these six men suggests, being a fitter in Port Talbot means being unemployed for much of the time. But the six men are not only all fitters, they have all experienced work with contracting firms at BSC. This book will explain how the quiet privatisation of BSC is largely to blame for the fact that Frank Clark and the others now suffer repeated spells of unemployment. Unemployment is the major theme of this book, but, despite its title, it is not a conventional study of mass unemployment. In large part this is due to the fact that Port Talbot — unlike Corby or Consett for example — did not lose its steelworks altogether as a result of BSC's attempts to rationalise steel production in the UK. Indeed, the second part of the book is concerned with the cost — to the people of Port Talbot — of *keeping* the steelworks in the town. Part of this cost has been the substitution of contractors for direct employment at BSC. This has produced mass '*under*-employment' (or 'sub-employment', see Norris, 1978), as well as mass unemployment. In the twilight world occupied by the contractors' workers it is often impossible to distinguish the unemployed from the employed. Numbers of workers, including skilled workers, have been introduced to a new form of employment: when in work they are aware that they will soon be out of work once more. This fact is just as important as the fact that in Port Talbot one in six people is out of work.

There is mass unemployment in Port Talbot. There are many people who are permanently out of work. But at any one time a substantial proportion of the unemployed will be made up of workers drawn from the under-employed group, those who can only expect to work for a part of each year and to be unemployed for the remainder. This is significant for the effect it has on these men and women when they are *in work*. Such workers — neither permanently employed nor permanently unemployed — are in a curious position. Any element of career choice has been removed and their lives are dominated by uncertainty and insecurity.

Before we begin to look at the consequences of under-employment, however, we need to fully understand its causes. We need to know how matters reached the stage (in 1980) when it was announced, albeit mistakenly, that Wales was closed.

**Footnotes**

1. See, for example, CIS, 1982; Le Grand and Robinson, 1984; Walker and Moore, 1983; see also *Guardian*, 20 June 1984 and, for the situation in South Wales, *Port Talbot Guardian*, 2 February 1984.

2. The problems of UK steel production have been analysed at length elsewhere and there is little to be gained from repeating the exercise here. Interested readers are recommended to look at Aylen, 1982, 1983; Bryer, Brignall and Maunders, 1982; Cottrell, 1981; Morgan, 1983; Upham, 1980.

3. All figures from ISTC Research Department.

4. By 1984 there were forty five small private mines in South Wales employing 600 miners and producing eight per cent of the total coal output of the region. Four or five applications for new workings were being received each month (*South Wales Evening Post*, 22 August 1984).

5. It appears that the Conservative Government approved of the increased use of private contractors as a method of privatisation: contractors have (more recently) been brought into the Inland Revenue, defence back-up industries, and the NHS (see, for example, *Guardian*, 20 June 1984, 3 April 1986 and 18 April 1986). The steel unions, in the person of the TUC Steel Committee, saw the use of contractors as a method of privatisation and suspected that politics as much as accounting (see Chapter Eight) had led BSC to increase its use of such contractors.

   Angela Coyle predicts that

   'The move towards the subcontracting of services to date has been the tip of the iceberg; it promises to be one of the most significant developments in the organisation of work over the next decade. This development is now being strategically planned by both Government and employers alike.'

   (Quoted in *Guardian*, 21 January 1987)

   Coyle found that the trend had been accelerated in the mid-1980s as a result of the Government's commitment to privatisation. The Labour Research Department reported that contracting out had already resulted in a net loss of 34,000 jobs in public services and predicted a further net decline of 129,000 jobs (*Guardian*, 21 January 1987).

Chapter Two

# Treasure Island and Slimline

*The Making of a Steeltown*

About half-an-hour's drive from Cardiff on the M4 going west, you come to a long, gentle bend where the landscape opens up unexpectedly to reveal the sweep of Swansea Bay and the distant cliffs of the Gower Peninsula. Don't blink if you want to savour this view because the road immediately straightens in the direction of Port Talbot. It enters a narrow strip of land which lies between the 'mountains' — only hills really — and the dunes. The strip is less than two miles wide at its narrowest point and it seems to be *full* of steelworks. The motorway runs parallel to five miles of coke ovens, strip mills and blast furnaces. If you drive through Port Talbot at night the impression is even stronger: on the right, the darkness of the mountains; on the left, pyrotechnics at the steelworks. The only suggestion of a town is the glimpse of rooftops from the slow lane of the elevated section of the motorway. This 'brutal road' passes through the town on stilts and it gives you little notion that people actually live here: you see a *steel town*, built for steel and not for people.

But there is another way to see Port Talbot. Walk to the top of Mynydd Emroch and look down. There is still a lot of steelworks and relatively few houses but you can see how the BSC site is contained and separated from the houses which surround it by the railway line (once the Great Western Railway) and the derelict land next to the tracks, more derelict land next to the old docks, and the docks themselves. Two sides of the site are water: the Bristol Channel and the docks. The water and the railway line make the steelworks an *island* in the town, 'Treasure Island' according to the people who found jobs there in the 1950s and 1960s.

The Abbey works at Port Talbot was built by the newly formed Steel Company of Wales (SCOW) after the war. SCOW was formed as a joint venture between two iron and steel producers with plants in Wales: Guest, Keen & Baldwins and Richard Thomas & Baldwins. Iron and steel had been produced in the town for some years. The old Port Talbot works were built in 1901 and the adjacent Margam works in 1916. Guest, Keen & Baldwins, formed in 1930, owned the old works (which employed 5,000 people). Planning for the new steelworks to the south began before the war but the announcement of a new plant, the Abbey works, and the modernisation and extension of the Margam works, was delayed until March 1947. Construction work began in the following month. A workforce of seven thousand — *plus* engineers, architects and so on — was used to complete 'this great British project' (*Iron and Coal Trades Review*, Special Issue, 1952).

The board of the Steel Company of Wales Ltd. was headed by Mr E.M. Lever and included Sir Charles Bruce-Gardner, Bt., Mr E. Julian Poole and Mr W.F. Cartwright. While the others were the financial movers behind SCOW[1], Cartwright was its engineer. He explained why Port Talbot was chosen as the site for the new steelworks:

> 'In the first place, South Wales has the largest reserves of coking coal in the United Kingdom and, therefore, on that score, the site was ideal. Another advantage was a port already developed with an iron ore wharf, a considerable amount of services available, a nucleus of trained personnel, sufficient water, good traffic access, and an enormous flat level site, unencumbered by any other buildings or indeed agricultural land of any material value. In addition, it is situated most favourably from a sociological point of view, being near a number of plants likely to become redundant.'
>
> (*Iron and Coal Trades Review*, Special Issue, 1952)

The people who used to work in these redundant plants were the first to see the Abbey works as their treasure island. They had once worked with what was virtually *hand*-technology and were now finding jobs in the most modern steelworks in Western Europe. Compared to their earlier jobs, the work at Port Talbot seemed like playtime and they were going to be paid what appeared to be a fortune to them. SCOW provided relatively high earnings and job security for a post-war generation. In addition to those who had worked in iron and steel, and in tinplate, in Port Talbot and the west, SCOW also recruited amongst the men who came from as far as Ireland to *build* the Abbey works. In later years many SCOW workers were recruited from the valleys as the pits were closed. Others came to look for work in Port Talbot from all over Britain, but it was not simply amongst those workers displaced by industrial change that new recruits were found. Treasure Island attracted craftsmen who had served their time in every trade and many others who gave up a job to work for SCOW: the self-employed gave up their shops and their funeral parlours and the policemen gave up their warrant cards.

SCOW was intended to supply jobs for adults, and wages were high enough to ensure that adults wanted the jobs. However, in the beginning SCOW also recruited numbers of local school-leavers. In 1951, 229 places for boys leaving school in Port Talbot were found in the steel industry. But SCOW's demand for school-leavers soon diminished and this was to prove a constant worry to the local Youth Employment Service (YES). In 1958 the Service complained that

'The Steel Company of Wales, with its problem of absorbing displaced workers from West Wales, has not been able to engage many boys, although there is a likelihood of more apprenticeships being offered during the next 12 months.'

In 1961, the YES pointed out that

'Although this is one of the largest centres in Europe for the steel industry the proportion of juveniles employed in it is small.'

Port Talbot was particularly short on jobs for school-leavers even then, and the YES repeated its complaints against SCOW throughout the 1960s. SCOW, in the meantime, reduced its recruitment of school-leavers still further. It was not until 1969 that prospects for school-leavers in Port Talbot improved but this was due to the opening of new factories and not to a change in recruitment policy at the steelworks.

On the specific point of *apprenticeships* for school-leavers, SCOW recruited about thirty apprentices each year in the 1950s. This increased to forty in 1959 with an increase in the ratio of apprentices to craftsmen (Glamorgan Education Authority 1950-1970). Opportunities for apprenticeships at the steelworks did not really begin to expand until the 1970s, however. Nevertheless, if you were 'lucky' enough to get an apprenticeship there in the early years — that is if you had a relative who worked for SCOW — the future held a great deal of promise. For example, if you got an apprenticeship in the Central Engineering Shop:

'The present craftsmen ... have generally come from one of three sources ...
'The third source is the most important, the company apprentice training scheme which has been designed to supply the future demand for craftsmen and technical staff for the various departments in the works. To ensure that the best is obtained both for the boys and the company, applicants for training are submitted to psychological tests for measuring their abilities, interests and personality traits. Discreet interpretation of the results of these tests plus the instructors' reports, guide a committee in advising the boys which particular craft or production field they should follow.
'Boys going in for mechanical engineering come to the school in the engineering workshops where they are trained in manual skills and machine operation. The school has been equipped with machine tools selected to ensure adequate training in all types of machine operation the boys are likely to meet in their subsequent careers, and has new machines of the most up-to-date patterns utilising the latest technological developments.

'Parallel with this practical training, the boys under their craft instructors receive lectures and demonstrations on the application of theoretical principles to their craft. They also attend day classes at the local technical colleges and are encouraged by incentives to pursue this training.

'To build up the quality of boys required to go forward as engineers and executives, the company has made available university scholarships. A committee consisting of representatives from the educational authorities and from the company management selects boys who have been submitted to them as a result of their practical and theoretical progress during their training.'

(*Iron and Coal Trades Review*, 1 October 1952)

In the 1950s the sky was apparently the limit for those, like some of the men mentioned in Chapter One, who had just completed their apprenticeships as fitters at the Abbey works. The sky seemed to be the limit for SCOW too. At its peak the company employed nearly 20,000 people, four times the current workforce of BSC Port Talbot. A man I shall call 'Derek Rees', one of the senior engineers who built and ran the steelworks until he retired in 1980, recalled the good old days in this way:

'... so what it half the employees didn't work? They [SCOW] were making money hand over fist, exported a third of their production and supplied BMC, Fords and the rest with the best and cheapest steel of its kind. That they had a bad reputation for delivery was understandable. They were like a Spanish hotel, overbooked since demand far exceeded supply ... And if they had a production bottleneck they simply took on more men, and more, and more, and more, up to the peak of 18,500 employees.'

Many of SCOW's workers commuted from Llanelli and the west and from the valleys. Others moved to Port Talbot, not just from Wales but from Ireland, Scotland and England as well, to houses on the new, and enormous, council estate which had been built for the steelworkers. Like the Abbey works, the estate was built on the flat land next to the dunes — but, mercifully, to the north of the town this time — and was of course christened *Sandfields*. The Council gave Sandfields homes for musicians, actors and poets: Bach Road, Brahms Avenue, Chopin Road, Elgar Avenue, Garrick House, Goya Place, Greig Close, Handel Avenue, Irving House, Lear House, Marlowe House, Mozart Avenue, Purcell Avenue, Verdi Road, Wagner Road. Even if you weren't lucky enough to live in a Novello House or a Strauss Road, there was, thanks to the Council, plenty of colour in the remaining streets — like Crimson Close, Golden Avenue and Scarlet Avenue. There were, however, no pubs. The Council seemed to think there were quite enough pubs in the town anyway and that there should be none on the Sandfields estate. Inspired by the Council, the residents founded their own social clubs. They could now do their drinking in the Bayview or the Seaside Social and Labour Club. The Seaside Club has little to do with the Labour Party but the residents of Sandfields, the workers of treasure island, filled the ranks of the local Labour Party just the same. They took over from the men of the Great Western Railway who had kept the local party on the tracks and soon they became councillors and some even became mayors. Before the 1950s had really got under way, Port Talbot had become a proper *steel town*; and what a town it was!

You might have called Port Talbot a 'frontier town' then: treasure island precipitated a sort of gold rush as people removed to the town in search of work and high wages. With the gold rush came the gambling: punters used express forms from the Post Office to make their illicit bets and Port Talbot used 50,000 of these forms every three months (*South Wales Evening Post*, 22 November 1983). It even, as befits a frontier town, had its own casino. But the high rollers in this town toted expense accounts rather than six-shooters and not all the poker games were at the casino. In 1973 the first issue of the magazine *Rebecca* was published. Until its premature demise, *Rebecca* fought to expose corruption in Wales. Looking through the back issues it seems that each of them could have been written solely on the basis of copy from Port Talbot. The town was in fact seen by the magazine's staff as a byword for the kind of practices they wished to expose. In 1975 Bob Dumbleton wrote:

'One of the great South Wales myths is that something nasty happened here in the last century and that ever since it has been hauling itself to recovery. Port Talbot is evidence that something nasty is still happening.

'Where shall we start the tour? In the east from what used to be the lovely, isolated beaches of Morfa Mawr now dredged to mud and soon to be reached by the waste lagoons of the British Steel Corporation? We could go by the motorway by-pass which by-passes the roofs by inches — a road described by one expert as "a brutal road, the cheapest solution".

'We should certainly visit where people live, in the great barracks of Sandfields, a foremost example of slum planning of the 1950s or in the even less fortunate workers' pre-war housing — or in the sodium dioxide suburb of Taibach — or where the private homeowners breath BP's more advanced gases in Baglan.

'We could stand at the centre of town and marvel at the very latest development: a new shopping shell for Woolworth and Tesco at the cost of a destroyed community, certain injury to its old people, a massive expenditure of public money (a permanent drain on the rates) and another new motorway, designed to deliver up the customers.

'We won't have time for everything — the Community Centre sold for bingo; the Lido that loses a million every year; the losing ride at the Miami Beach funfair. We could end at the sad seafront (the miner's day out!) going to the higest bidders. And as we contemplate the polluted waves wonder at it all.

'For riches were promised to Port Talbot. And delivered in the shape of the steelworks, the chemical works, the town centre redevelopment. So how come those riches are heavy labour, job insecurity, danger and ill-health in a place like that? Riches boiled down to the simple prayer "thank god it isn't Ebbw Vale".

'I have this feeling that Port Talbot is the big clue. If we understood how it all gears together — giant state industry, international and local business, council and government, officials and professions and trade unions — how together it all composes the tragic mess of Port Talbot — then we would understand all we ever need to know of politics and economics — the complex simplicity of wealth and power ...

'Already we can see ... Port Talbot as a political machine for converting public assets into private profit. We can see that beggars for capital never become choosers over capital after life-times of work. And running through all this — what the Labour Party is or has become. It is a haunting old story of socialism that never was and the price we pay for its absence.

'I hope to follow the clue of Port Talbot in future articles. Perhaps you will join us? Who knows, we may find Port Talbot everywhere.' (*Rebecca*, July-August, 1975)[2]

This piece tells us the price that some people paid for the 'easy money' they earned at the steelworks in Port Talbot: *they had to live there*.

The 'great British project' had costs as well as benefits: living in Port Talbot was one of the costs but other costs became apparent after SCOW became part of BSC in 1967. The engineer, Derek Rees, blamed nationalisation itself: with nationalisation 'the steam went out of Port Talbot'. Local people were no longer allowed to make decisions: some took years to make, some were never made, and morale declined. Moreover, management was no longer accessible, or, rather, the managers who mattered were no longer accessible. You could get to see the people in Port Talbot but they had to answer to the divisional (Wales) management, and the divisional managers had, in turn, to answer to London. There was no longer any local control over engineering decisions, let alone decisions concerning capital investment.

More importantly, employment at the steelworks began to fall. Table 2.1 shows that peak employment at SCOW had been reached in 1960 when 18,352 people were employed there, but the steelworks still employed 16,754 people when it was nationalised. By 1979, however, BSC Port Talbot's total workforce had dropped

**Table 2.1 SCOW and BSC Port Talbot 'Actual Manning'\* 1948-1985**

| 1948[1] | 4,337 | 1963 | 17,847 | 1978 | 12,555 |
|---|---|---|---|---|---|
| 1949 | 4,452 | 1964 | 17,764 | 1979 | |
| 1950[2] | 4,863 | 1965 | 17,487 | (29 Sept) | 12,584 |
| 1951 | 7,441 | 1966 | 16,762 | (end Nov) | 12,468 |
| 1952 | 9,071 | 1967[4] | 16,754 | (end Dec) | 12,415 |
| 1953[3] | 10,063 | 1968 | 15,531 | 1980 | |
| 1954 | 11,051 | 1969 | 14,884 | (16 May) | 11,486 |
| 1955 | 12,390 | 1970 | 14,725 | (end June) | 11,259 |
| 1956 | 13,754 | 1971 | 14,029 | (end Dec) | 6,636 |
| 1957 | 14,824 | 1972 | 13,642 | 1981 | 5,626 |
| 1958 | 15,497 | 1973 | 13,812 | 1982 | 5,319 |
| 1959 | 17,627 | 1974 | 14,053 | 1983 | 4,797 |
| 1960 | 18,352 | 1975 | 13,492 | 1984 | 4,808 |
| 1961 | 17,790 | 1976 | 13,140 | 1985 | 4,746[5] |
| 1962 | 18,006 | 1977 | 13,139 | | |

\* End of December except where stated. Vacancies, part-timers and temporaries included. Research and Development staff excluded from 1968 (total r & d of 308 in 1968).

**Notes**
1. SCOW formed.
2. Nationalisation.
3. De-nationalisation.
4. Nationalisation.
5. Estimated figure.

**Source:** BSC Port Talbot Personnel Department.

to 12,584.[3] Yet despite falling employment at the steelworks, Port Talbot was *more* dependent on BSC for jobs at the end of the 1970s than it had been at the beginning of the decade.

Full details of employment in Port Talbot are available elsewhere (Fevre, 1984a) but there is space here for a summary of the main trends. In 1971 BSC provided thirty six per cent of Port Talbot's jobs but by 1978 this figure had risen to thirty nine per cent. Since we know that employment at BSC actually fell over this period it is clear that total employment in Port Talbot must have fallen at a faster rate. Table 2.2 shows that Port Talbot lost 7,400 jobs between 1971 and 1978. The decline in employment in Port Talbot from just over 39,000 to just under 32,000 meant that one in five of the town's jobs had disappeared before the decade was out. The table shows that most of the jobs were lost in the construction industry, where employment declined from 8,600 in 1971 to 3,100 in 1978, but mechanical engineering was also badly hit.

BSC saved Port Talbot in the 1970s. It did the same job that growth industries, particularly in the service sector, did in the rest of

**Table 2.2 Employees in Employment in the Port Talbot Employment Office Area 1971-1978\* (in thousands)**

|  | 1971 | 1972 | 1973 | 1974 | 1975 | 1976 | 1977 | 1978 |
|---|---|---|---|---|---|---|---|---|
| *Primary Industries (orders I-II)* | 0.3 | 0.2 | 0.6 | 0.2 | 0.1 | 0.1 | 0.1 | 0.1 |
| *Manufacturing (orders III-XIX)* | 21.5 | 20.8 | 20.6 | 21.9 | 21.2 | 20.2 | 19.7 | 19.1 |
| *Construction (order XX)* | 8.6 | 6.1 | 3.8 | 3.3 | 3.2 | 4.1 | 4.0 | 3.1 |
| *All Services and Public Administration (orders XXI-XXVII)* | 9.0 | 8.9 | 9.1 | n/a[1] | 8.5 | 8.8 | 8.9 | 9.3 |
| **TOTAL** *All Industries and Services* | 39.2 | 36.1 | 33.9 | n/a[1] | 33.1 | 33.3 | 32.8 | 31.8 |

\* June of each year.

**Note**
1. Public Administration figures not available due to local government reorganisation.

**Source:** Department of Employment.

Britain. Take the county in which Port Talbot is situated, West Glamorgan. Iron and Steel was the major employer in West Glamorgan in 1978 but fully three-quarters of these jobs were in Port Talbot (as against twenty per cent of all West Glamorgan's employment). Once iron and steel were excluded, the pattern of employment in West Glamorgan looked much more normal: manufacturing had declined throughout the 1970s but this had been compensated by growth in the service sector. Total employment in West Glamorgan actually increased as a result, and by 1978 thirty nine per cent of male employment and eighty per cent of female employment was in the service sector. Table 2.3 shows that in Port Talbot the service sector provided only eighteen per cent of male jobs and sixty eight per cent of female jobs. Services and public administration were the only sectors of employment in Port Talbot where the numbers of employees actually increased but table 2.2 shows that only 300 extra jobs were created in these sectors between 1971 and 1978. Service sector growth was so insignificant in Port Talbot that the proportion of the town's male jobs in *manufacturing*

**Table 2.3 Male and Female Employees in Employment in the Port Talbot Employment Office Area and West Glamorgan June 1978 (percentages)**

|  | MEN | | WOMEN | |
|---|---|---|---|---|
|  | Port Talbot % | West Glamorgan % | Port Talbot % | West Glamorgan % |
| Primary Industries | 0.4 | 5.7 | 0.0 | 0.5 |
| Manufacturing | 69.3 | 45.3 | 31.1 | 19.1 |
| Construction | 12.3 | 10.5 | 1.4 | 0.9 |
| Gas, Electricity etc. | 0.0 | 1.7 | 0.0 | 0.6 |
| Distributive Trades | 2.9 | 6.7 | 16.2 | 16.8 |
| Miscellaneous Services | 2.0 | 5.2 | 14.9 | 12.1 |
| Public Administration | 4.1 | 7.9 | 6.8 | 15.0 |
| Other Service Industries | 8.6 | 17.1 | 29.7 | 35.0 |

**Source:** Department of Employment.

was actually higher in 1978 than 1971.

As before, Port Talbot's steelworks produced both costs and benefits for the town. As late as 1978, Port Talbot owed its superficial appearance of health to BSC, but the foregoing discussion has shown that the town's reliance on manufacturing and construction made it vulnerable and so did its reliance on steel. The bias towards steel had served to insulate Port Talbot from the worst ravages of manufacturing decline in the 1970s but from 1978 things began to change.

On 15th May 1980 BSC signed an agreement with the trade unions which was called 'Slimline'. Slimline involved the loss of 5,549 jobs over the period July to December 1980. Total employment at BSC Port Talbot was to be reduced from 11,259 (the figure for the end of June) to 5,701. The number of job losses under Slimline was simply staggering, something totally out of the ordinary run of events. But it was not simply the size of the cuts that was out of the ordinary, the way they were brought about was also something new.

*How Slimline was 'Agreed'*

Apart from the size of the job losses it produced, Slimline differed in three important respects from anything that had gone before. Firstly it was the government that initiated the rationalisation process. Secondly, BSC Port Talbot was actually threatened with closure in order to make local management come up with an appropriate rationalisation plan. Thirdly, the cuts were not negotiated with the relevant trade unions. Right up to the end of

1979 BSC and the unions were still engaged in open collective bargaining but Slimline was forced through by a mixture of confrontation and secret deals with union officials. In order to understand just how abnormal Slimline was — in every respect — we have to know something of what went before.

Nearly 6,000 jobs had been lost at BSC Port Talbot since 1960 but Port Talbot had never seen anything on the scale of the 1980 redundancies. Many of these earlier job losses had been brought about by not filling vacancies and through natural wastage. There were no large redundancies until 1986 and these were achieved through the normal process of collective bargaining. The craft productivity agreement of 1968 brought about 400 job losses, however only a proportion of these involved redundancies and all of them were voluntary. Voluntary redundancies and natural wastage also accounted for the disappearance of over 2,000 jobs in 1970 and 1971 when the Abbey melting shop was closed. In subsequent years, especially from 1976, employment was gradually reduced as a result of BSC's efforts to cut jobs throughout the UK. None of these losses involved 'hard' redundancies, that is, all of the redundants chose to leave. This was still the case in 1978 when the Work Measurement Incentive Scheme (WMIS) brought about 600 job losses amongst process workers including some (voluntary) redundancies.

In 1979 BSC was still 'paring away at manning' according to the Port Talbot managers. Negotiations with the staff unions (including process and craft foremen) under the Fixed Cost Reductions scheme had been completed by August 1979 but not implemented. Similarly, a Group Working Practices agreement with the craftsmen was concluded (but not implemented) in September. The projected loss of 1,000 staff jobs through Fixed Cost Reductions and of 200 craft jobs through the Group Working Practices agreement would appear to be a continuation, in what turned out to be a period of major changes in output, production strategy and employment policy, of the attempt to reduce labour costs which BSC has been making since 1976. They occurred in the 'normal course of business' as normality was defined in the 1970s (House of Commons Committee on Welsh Affairs, 1980). Upon this 'normal course' a quite different set of considerations was imposed however.

In 1979 the Government got tough with BSC, or rather two governments got tough. The outgoing Labour Government told BSC to do something about its 'over-capacity'. The Conservative Government (which came in with the general election of May 1979) told BSC that it could not have as much money from the Government as it would like and that operating losses would no longer be funded. Throughout 1979, therefore, 'normal' consultations about 'normal' job loss were accompanied by managerial explorations of an abnormal reduction in employment, leading to substantial redundancy. BSC was on course for large-scale redundancy far removed from that envisaged in the context of 1970s normalcy.

BSC's first attempt at rationalisation was a plan called *The Radical Review* which had been set in train by the outgoing Labour Government. In September 1979 the (Conservative) Secretary of State for Industry, Sir Keith Joseph rejected *The Radical Review*. The Government did not think the plan was radical enough and told BSC to get rid of at least 50,000 jobs from their workforce of 186,000. BSC did eventually come up with a cut of 50,000 (in fact a little more) in November 1979. According to ISTC's 'New Deal for Steel', this was when the Chief Executive of BSC, Bob Scholey, produced the plan which was later to become *The Return to Financial Viability* (BSC, 1979).

*The Return to Financial Viability* laid out the 'plant configurations' necessary for BSC to meet the Government's financial requirements. It envisaged 52,000 job losses and total BSC output of fifteen million tonnes of steel per annum. Although Wales as a whole was covered by the plan, it did not say exactly how the Welsh cuts were to be achieved. The production of the two Welsh plants, Llanwern (near Newport) and Port Talbot, was to be cut from a combined total of 4.6 million tonnes to 2.7 million tonnes, however the plan presented four alternative ways of achieving this aim. Firstly the Port Talbot workforce could be reduced and the Llanwern plant closed. Secondly, both plants would stay open but employment would be reduced at both. This would necessitate a bigger cut in the Port Talbot workforce than under option one since Port Talbot would make 1.4 million tonnes of steel (as against 2.7) with Llanwern making the rest. Similar cuts in employment at both plants would be needed for the third alternative, what BSC called the 'dog leg'. Under this option both plants would be partially closed: Port Talbot would lose its capacity to roll steel strip and Llanwern would no longer make steel. Port Talbot would produce the steel (in the form of slabs) for Llanwern to role into strip. The final option was the reverse of the first: Port Talbot would close and the 2.7 million tonnes would be produced by Llanwern alone.

In November 1979 the Director of BSC Port Talbot was told about the four alternatives and informed the Port Talbot management committee. He told them they must produce a plan for option two — steelmaking and rolling to continue at both plants but on a reduced scale — since this was the only realistic way to save the plant. He did not think BSC would close Llanwern and the dog-leg alternative would amount to 'slow closure' of Port Talbot.

According to members of the Port Talbot management committee the details for option two were worked out in December. Each manager was asked how many jobs they could lose if production was cut from 2.3 to 1.4 million tonnes of steel per annum. Furthermore, each manager was under pressure from his (there were no women members of the committee) colleagues to name the lowest possible figure for his part of the plant. Their first estimates were high but the Director conducted a Dutch auction which forced each manager down to the lowest number of employees with which he thought he could run the part of the plant for which he was responsible. Each single job which was to be cut was personally approved by the Director. A few minor changes — in the form of job-swapping between departments — took place later on, but the final employment figure for production at 1.4 million tonnes was reached in December. The figure that the Port Talbot managers came up with was 5,701. BSC Port Talbot's workforce at this time was 12,415.

As it turned out, events had moved rather too quickly for the Port Talbot managers because *The Return to Financial Viability* went to the BSC Board without a final decision on the South Wales plants. The Board approved the plan on the 10th December. From this date all the BSC managers except those at Llanwern and Port Talbot knew their 'plant configurations' (although some employment figures were still being 'refined'). So that complete financial calculations could be given to the Board, *The Return to Financial Viability* had assumed that the dog-leg alternative would be adopted in South Wales. This might still be the favoured option because any alternative would have to produce similar, or better, savings:

> 'the precise configuration should be left for determination when the Welsh Division has produced final proposals within these parameters:
>
> (a)  That the steel output of the Welsh Strip Mills should be the 2.7 million tonnes per annum indicated in this paper;
>
> (b)  That the solution should not adversely affect the results postulated for the Scottish and Teeside divisions; and
>
> (c)  That the Welsh Division achieves at Port Talbot and Llanwern *at least the profit projection incorporated in this assessment.*'
>
> (BSC, 1979, emphasis added)

The job of deciding which option would be adopted for South Wales was given to Peter Allen, Managing Director of the Welsh Division. He was asked

> 'to recommend to the Board the course of action which should be taken,

as to how best the 2.8 [sic] million tonnes should be made at the two plants in South Wales.'

(House of Commons Committee on Welsh Affairs, 1980)

At Port Talbot the Director told his managers and the unions that he would try to persuade BSC to accept option one (Port Talbot producing 2.7 million tonnes, Llanwern closed). For this option Port Talbot would offer a workforce of 7,000. This proposal was turned down, as expected, but the Director's second choice of 5,701 workers making 1.4 million tonnes was accepted. A similar 'Slimline' solution was adopted for Llanwern.[4]

The Port Talbot managers had done enough in their December planning to satisfy BSC. 'Done enough' meant losing enough jobs. Slimline was clearly not the most productive of the four alternatives (BSC, 1980). For example, overall productivity under Slimline at Port Talbot would be only two-thirds of the level which Port Talbot could offer under option one if Llanwern was closed. Yet Slimline met BSC's requirements. Before the January meeting BSC knew exactly how many jobs would have to go in South Wales if they were to meet their target since job losses elsewhere had already been decided. In fact the Director of BSC Port Talbot may have been told exactly how many jobs were to be cut if Slimline were to be accepted. Members of the management committee reported that such a figure was never mentioned to them but said that the Director may have had this target in mind and simply stopped pressing them for more cuts when it was achieved.

The Slimline proposals were accepted by the BSC Board on 17th January 1980 but the majority of workers affected by them knew nothing of BSC's plans for another couple of weeks. They were occupied with other concerns: on the 17th January they were beginning their fifteenth day of a national steel strike — about pay, not jobs — which would last for another two-and-a-half months.

With hindsight the way BSC handled the cuts in steel appears to be a prototype for the tactics used by management to effect reductions in other nationalised industries, a sort of rehearsal for the coal dispute of 1984/5.[5] It appears that BSC goaded the unions into a strike which would demoralise the workforce and leave them with no fight left to resist redundancies.

The steel pay talks broke down on 3rd December 1979 after BSC offered the workers a pay increase which was so low that ISTC — which had never had a national strike — resolved to take industrial action. *The Return to Financial Viability* — with its 52,000 job losses — was accepted by the BSC Board three days after the ISTC Executive Council instructed all BSC members to strike. It is almost as if BSC had to wait for the strike call before finalising their

rationalisation plans. In any event ISTC were more reluctant than
BSC to enter a dispute since ISTC postponed the date of industrial
action until 2nd January. BSC was able to use the month's notice of
strike action to add to their stocks of steel. Union sources at Port
Talbot claim that stocks were already higher than normal in the
Autumn of 1979 when BSC was ordering extra shifts and paying
overtime to its workers.

Furthermore, it was BSC which made jobs an issue in the strike.
This was entirely BSC's choice since the unions had considered the
possibilities and rejected it. On the 10th January the TUC's Steel
Committee — made up of all the leaders of the unions with
members in the industry — decided not to bring BSC's threat to
jobs into the dispute.[6] BSC had no qualms about making the strikers
aware of the threat to their jobs, and thus risking a longer dispute.
BSC effectively raised the stakes shortly after the unions had
dismissed the idea when they made it clear that any settlement of
the strike would mean the workers' acceptance of the loss of 52,000
jobs.[7]

The rest of the story of the ninety-two day steel strike is well-
known. The workers returned, beaten and demoralised, after their
unions had accepted an offer so unsatisfactory as to allow little face-
saving. They then offered no resistance to BSC's redundancy plans.
Yet this story does not apply to *all* BSC's workers because while the
*public* drama was being played out some of BSC's employees were
engaged in *secret* talks with their employer.

Secret talks about large-scale redundancies at Port Talbot began
shortly after Sir Keith Joseph rejected *The Radical Review*. In the
Autumn of 1979 BSC were discussing 3,000 redundancies at Port
Talbot, and other economies, 'with a small number of Trade
Unionists in the plant in confidence' (House of Commons
Committee on Welsh Affairs, 1980). Unfortunately news of these
talks was soon leaked to the press (*Western Mail*, 23 November
1979), much to the displeasure of the Department of Trade and
Industry.

When it became clear that the size of the cuts BSC planned to
make would have to be increased, BSC told a (larger) number of
trade union officials at Port Talbot about the four alternatives for
South Wales (House of Commons Committee on Welsh Affairs,
1980). According to the Port Talbot management these talks took
place in the first week of December 1979. Later in December, after
the management committee had worked out the detailed plans for
Slimline, the multi-union committee at Port Talbot was told exactly
what would happen — 'each job which would go' — if their
submission for option two was successful.

BSC called this series of talks 'consultations' rather than

negotiations, but even the term consultation gives a misleading impression of the union officials' role. According to both sides at the talks in Port Talbot, the union officials were simply present to be *told* what was going to happen. They were *told* that Slimline was the best they could hope for and they were *told* exactly how Slimline would be achieved — none of the details of Slimline were negotiable.[8]

Slimline was accepted by the BSC Board on 17th January 1980 but this was not the end of the 'consultations'. On that date the Board announced that they had decided to concentrate further discussions 'with the unions and workforce' on the Slimline option. The Board had also decided that 'consultations' on Slimline would have to be concluded by 31st March 1980 so that Slimline could be operational by August. At first sight this seems a little strange since the 'unions and workforce' were actually out on strike at the time 'consultations' were supposed to take place. In fact there is no confusion: the union officials at Port Talbot took time off from organising the strike to talk to their employers about the best way to make 5,000 of their members redundant. As one trade union employee (not a trade union official) put it:

'While we were marching outside, some of the branch officers were inside negotiating redundancies.'

In one sense this is literally true. Although the jobs which were to be lost at Port Talbot had been specified by the management committee in December, the managers didn't know which workers were going to be made redundant. To complete the planning for the implementation of Slimline at the end of the strike they needed the unions' help:

'We determined which jobs were to go; then we had a procedure with each union to decide which worker was to go.'

Most unions had an established (compulsory) redundancy procedure, usually 'last-in-first-out', and produced lists of members in order of seniority. Others had to be threatened in order to produce lists of redundants. Thus BSC said they would simply send out notices to current job-holders 'to get the intransigent unions' cooperation'. Of course not all of the workers listed by the unions as redundants were in jobs which BSC had earmarked to go. The solution to this problem was 'cross-matching', a process which transferred the workers who were to stay to safe jobs. Cross-matching was also used *after* the strike to transfer volunteers for redundancy to jobs which were to be shed.[9]

The remaining 'consultations' between the Port Talbot

management committee and the Port Talbot multi-union committee during the steel strike concerned severance payments and pay. Enhanced severance payments are usually used to buy union cooperation in redundancies, however at Port Talbot cooperation came cheaply and the unions had little success in forcing up severance payments before BSC's deadline of 31st March. They were still trying in April, however, but the members of the multi-union committee were forced to ask their respective union leaders for help. The leaders were asked to visit the works, as the TUC Steel Committee, in order to negotiate a higher ex-gratia severance payment.

It is hard to believe that the union officials at Port Talbot were talking to their employers about pay during a national pay strike, but an agreement on a local production bonus at Port Talbot *was* reached before the strike ended. The fact that such local agreements were only allowed, for the first time, by the national agreement which ended the strike seems to have made no difference to managers and union officials at Port Talbot. It is not at all clear, however, that the local union officials gained by agreeing to a local production bonus. Subsequent events at Port Talbot suggest that local officials were mistaken if they believed this. BSC had wanted local productivity agreements for some time and plant-based productivity bargaining proved as divisive in steel as in coal: local management was able to bring up a series of proposals for further cutbacks at each set of annual negotiations over these productivity payments. The unions found that productivity bargaining allowed management to make any pay increase dependent on further job losses.

Consultations with the trade unions at Port Talbot took place during the steel strike because Port Talbot management was under instructions from BSC to complete these talks by the 31st March. (Management had already given the necessary notice of the redundancies which were planned for March when they notified the Department of Employment in January). Managers used the March date as a deadline in their talks with trade union officials at the plant. Nevertheless, no agreement could be put into operation before the end of the strike and so BSC subsequently revised their timetable. As the strike dragged on BSC decided that consultations should be completed by the end of June so that Slimline could be fully operational by December.[10]

In fact consultations at Port Talbot *were* completed by the end of March and, although the Slimline Agreement was not signed until May, some parts of the Agreement were put into operation *before the end of the strike*. Thus some BSC Port Talbot employees were made redundant before the dispute was settled on the 1st of April.

The strikers returned to work on the 3rd April and it was only then that the majority of BSC workers learned what the rumours of redundancy would actually mean for them. They learned the details from their trade union officials. The officials had to secure the agreement of their members before they could sign the Slimline Agreement. They did this in branch meetings throughout April. One TGWU branch was still rejecting Slimline (by 150 votes to 6) on 22nd April but agreement had been reached in all trade union branches by May.

The Slimline Agreement between management and unions at Port Talbot was signed on 15th May 1980. It looks very much like the plan put before the BSC Board on 17th January by the Chief Executive, but with the addition of a local productivity agreement. Under Slimline 5,549 jobs would be cut. This would reduce the workforce to 5,701 from a total of 11,250. (This was the 'authorised' rather than '*actual* manning' figure: it assumed that the cuts planned from the previous year — under the Fixed Cost Reductions and Group Working Practices arrangements — had already taken place). The figure of 5,701 was to be the 'authorised manning' for production of 1.4 million tonnes of steel per annum.

In public, at least, the leaders of the trade unions concerned claimed only to have heard about this Agreement (and the complementary Slimline Agreement for Llanwern) a month before it was signed.[11] This seems less than likely since they had known about BSC's plans to reduce employment in South Wales since December 1979 when they received a copy of *The Return to Financial Viability* before it went to the BSC Board for approval. Furthermore, some union employees, the local full-time officers of the unions, had been informed of the Slimline 'consultations' by the Director of BSC Port Talbot on the 20th December. We must remember, however, that the leaders of at least one union were reluctant to make jobs a strike issue.

The distinction between trade union officials and trade union *officers* is an important one, although difficult to make since the terms are sometimes used as equivalents and there seems to be no general agreement as to when each term should be used. I will use the term 'officials' to refer to lay members of the union who have been *elected* to some position of authority at branch level and possibly also to higher union bodies including the national decision-making body, for example the ISTC's Executive Council. 'Officers' are the unions' paid professionals. They work as employees of the union in its regional or national offices. (In the case of ISTC, divisional officers are appointed by the Executive Council rather than elected by the lay membership). For whatever reason, the local full-time union officers were excluded from the Slimline consultations by the elected union officials at Port Talbot (although not at Llanwern). In fact these officials *never* informed the union officers of their talks with management. The only proper notification the officers received was from BSC. For example, on 11th April one full-timer received a copy of the Slimline 'proposal' from Peter Allen, Managing Director of the Welsh Division.

Unfortunately for the union leaders, especially the leadership of ISTC, the matter was not laid to rest after the Slimline Agreement was signed. In part their continuing discomfort resulted from the intervention of the Wales TUC. At the meeting of the TUC Steel Committee on 2nd June 1980,

> 'The letter, dated May 19, from the Welsh TUC to Mr Murray was then read. It asked the General Secretary to intervene personally, together with the Steel Committee, to get the agreement which had recently been reached in BSC's slimline proposals withdrawn. It claimed that the agreement had been made by ISTC members without any consultation with other unions or full-time officers and would have serious consequences for Wales...
>
> 'In a lengthy discussion it was noted that a similar agreement on Slimline had been made at Llanwern the previous week. Various views were then expressed about how the agreement came to be made — an ISTC representative said that tremendous pressure had been exerted by certain ISTC members of Port Talbot to get an agreement signed, and the Chairman remarked that under ISTC's constitution the membership had the right to take this line —; the reasons underlying it, the divisive tactics of the management; and whether or not any union, or the Committee, as such, could or should have tried to prevent the agreement from being concluded [sic]. It was generally agreed that each union concerned at Port Talbot should let the office have a statement of its view about how the agreement came to be made...'

ISTC was obliged to take some sort of action in the wake of pressure from other unions and the Welsh TUC and so some branch officials at Port Talbot were disciplined, however this did little to heal the breach between elected officials and union officers caused by the exclusion of full-timers from the Slimline consultations. For some time after the Slimline Agreement was signed, there was no working relationship between full-timers (in London or South Wales) and local union branches. The cold war continued for three years, during which time the local officials could not rely on full-timers or the national office for support, and the latter had no trust in the Port Talbot officials. Some of the officials who had offended were subsequently removed and the division was reorganised with new full-timers appointed to look after the interests of the workers at Port Talbot.

ISTC officers now claim that the union would be able to prevent local deals like Slimline,[12] but the lasting effect of BSC's twin tactics of confrontation and secret deals was to divide and break trade union organisation at Port Talbot, especially ISTC's. One BSC Port Talbot manager was able to say that 'the unions came out of [Slimline] with a lot of credit' but after Slimline the unions did not have a lot of credit with their members, or a lot of power. The effects of the Slimline debacle handicapped the Port Talbot unions in all their dealings with management (and not just *BSC* management) in subsequent years.

### Footnotes

1. Finance was unproblematic since it was clear that the technology currently in use was obsolete and that there was a ready market for sheet steel, especially the wider strip which Port Talbot would produce and which would be used to make cars, fridges and so on.

2. The reference to Ebbw Vale is to another Welsh steelworks where 1,276 redundancies were announced in 1975. On the subject of corruption in Port Talbot, *Rebecca* was able to break the news in 1978 of a massive scandal in the allocation of contracts for the 'redevelopment' of the town centre. Three of the councillors named in the article were steelworkers. The subsequent corruption trial turned out to be one of the longest in British legal history and a record fine was imposed on a local firm of civil engineering contractors, of whom more later. In the world of 1970s corruption, of property booms and urban redevelopment, Port Talbot was amongst the league leaders. The town even played a minor role in the Norman Scott affair.

3. All BSC employment figures, including actual employment figures, were supplied by BSC Port Talbot Personnel Department.

4. According to the union officials who signed the Llanwern Slimline Agreement, events at their plant did not proceed in quite the same way as at Port Talbot. They claim that BSC had decided on total or partial (dog-leg) closure for Llanwern late in 1978 (*before* the general election). *Some* senior managers at Llanwern wanted to save the plant, however, and told them of the existence of a 'Slimline' option for BSC's other strip mills. The union officials were happy to grasp at this straw and, with the help of these managers, put Llanwern's figures into the Slimline format. Management then successfully argued their case with BSC. The Llanwern Slimline Agreement — signed slightly later than its Port Talbot equivalent — reduced 'authorised manning' at the plant from 9,353 to 4,899.

5. During the strike the steelworkers didn't need the benefit of hindsight. A cartoon in the ISTC journal pictured the Prime Minister talking to Bob Scholey, BSC's Chief Executive, dressed as a Mafia godfather. Mrs Thatcher is saying

   'After we've sorted out the Iron and Steel industry, Bob, do you think you and your godsons could take out a contract on the miners for me?' (*Man and Metal*, January/February 1980).

   The cartoonist was mistaken of course: it was the Chairman of BSC, Mr Ian Macgregor, and not the Chief Executive, who went on to the National Coal Board.

6. There is some suggestion that ISTC, of all the relevant unions, were the most reluctant to do this. Indeed, union sources report that ISTC were consistently opposed to striking over jobs. Some of the craft unions are believed to have favoured delaying any strike action until the summer of 1980 when, after an

overtime ban, BSC workers would have taken action over jobs, not pay. In fact the only attempt to mount a general campaign against redundancies took place (at a later date) in *South Wales* (Morgan, 1983: 192).

7. Reported in Granada Television's *World in Action* programme of 4th February 1980. As a result of BSC's initiative, Gavin Laird (AUEW), Bill Sirs (ISTC) and other members of the TUC Nationalised Industries Committee met the Chancellor of the Exchequer and the Secretaries of State for Industry and Employment on 31st January 1980 to discuss the proposed employment reductions (and especially their effects in South Wales).

8. This suggests that BSC's evidence to the Welsh Committee was — perhaps unintentionally — misleading. In evidence to the Committee, Peter Allen said that

'The full consultation with trade union officials at the works showed that the "Slimline" option seemed to be the most acceptable.'

This surely implies that the union officials had some choice in the matter?

9. Cross-matching had been used in 1970/1 to transfer workers who volunteered for redundancy to the Abbey melting shop where redundancies were planned.

10. Rather than August. In fact Slimline was not fully operational until 1981, see Chapter Three.

11. Minutes of TUC Steel Committee meeting of 8th April 1980.

12. In February 1983 six ISTC officials at BSC Port Talbot were dismissed from their posts by the South Wales divisional officer because they tried to negotiate a local pay deal, but 'an ISTC spokesman' at the plant claimed the ban on local talks had been an ISTC recommendation and not an instruction (*South Wales Evening Post*, 14 February 1983). Two months later the six men were reinstated to their positions in the union following pressure from local branches (*Port Talbot Guardian*, 21 April 1983).

Chapter Three

# Treasure Island Becomes 'Giro City'

*The Year Of The Redundancies*

It has been said that the people of Wales are accustomed to using the past as a point of reference for the present and the future — look at their history of trade union and Labour Party politics, their 'tight' communities and the single industries, coal and steel, on which these communities were based. It is not simply that history *explains* what comes next, but that it helps to *shape* it: through the past we make our future[1]. To an extent this was also true of the people of Port Talbot, but the events of 1980 seemed to thoroughly destroy any link with the past for many people in the town. The scale of the collapse meant that what came next could no longer in any way resemble what had gone before.

Before Christmas 1979 the steelworks in Port Talbot was planning 'normal' reductions in employment but was still expected to have a workforce of 11,250 in the following year. Production at BSC was actually to be increased from 2.3 million tonnes capacity at the end of 1979 to 2.7 million tonnes in 1980. By May 1980 BSC had decided the works was going to be producing 1.4 million tonnes with 5,701 employees.

In fact the figure of 5,701, the 'authorised manning' level for Slimline, was *not* reached by the end of 1980. The workforce of BSC Port Talbot was reduced from 12,415 in December 1979 to 6,636 a year later (see table 2.1). The total job losses in 1980 therefore amounted to 5,779 but 1,230 of these jobs were accounted for by the cuts planned under the Fixed Cost Reductions and Group Working Practices agreements of 1979. Full implementation of Slimline, involving another 1,000 job losses, took place over the next four years (and so overlapped with later job losses through further rationalisation).

Almost all of the 5,779 job losses in 1980 involved redundancies. The workers still to be made redundant under Fixed Cost Reductions were the first to go. A BSC manager described these redundancies as the worst of all: 'the most savage agreement, all hard redundancies'. They were followed by the remaining redundancies under the Group Working Practices agreement and, finally, by the 4,500 Slimline redundancies. According to figures supplied by the Manpower Services Commission, the majority of these redundancies had occurred by 11th September 1980. (The

MSC figures for September suggest that only 2.5 per cent of the redundants were women, and although this proportion increased a little in subsequent months, the vast majority of the Slimline redundants were men. Larger numbers of women were made redundant, however, as a result of the earlier agreements which dealt with clerical employment).

For many, inside and outside Wales, Port Talbot became the symbol of the disaster that befell British manufacturing industry and the people who worked in it, in 1980. Much more than other BSC redundancies at Shotton, or even Ebbw Vale, it was the Port Talbot redundancies that captured the imagination of TV producers and feature writers. Perhaps they remembered the 'great British project' from their 'A' level geography textbooks, or perhaps the attraction was geographical in a more literal sense. You could catch a train at Paddington in mid-morning and walk out of Port Talbot station into the Grand for lunch. Later you could chat up the assistant in the estate agent's office (about falling property prices), visit one of the houses in the shadow of the blast furnaces, take a picture of the graffiti in the bus shelters, and still be home in Hampstead for dinner.

Thanks perhaps to British Rail, Port Talbot became a national symbol, just as *Rebecca* had once hoped. This Port Talbot of the mind reached its melodramatic limits in a feature film which used the symbol to tie together tales of recession, corruption and skullduggery. As we have seen, Port Talbot was not short on any of these, but the film was hardly meant to be a factual account and the only things it took from the town were some images of dreariness and depression. Moreover Port Talbot is a *town* and the film was called 'Giro *City*' but the label was appropriate all the same. In 1980 it really did seem as if Port Talbot was going to become a town populated solely by unemployed people waiting for delivery of the Post Office Giros which paid their welfare benefits. For one thing, BSC was not the only firm which had announced redundancies.

Far from being in a position to compensate for the reduction in employment in steel by creating *new* jobs, other Port Talbot employers were also shedding workers. The official figures on redundancies[2] show that the rate of contraction in employment in Port Talbot accelerated after 1978, reaching a peak in 1980. While the number of redundancies increased throughout West Glamorgan, it was in Port Talbot that the most severe contraction took place. In 1978 the town had about twenty per cent of all the *jobs* in the county but between January 1976 and June 1980 Port Talbot experienced fifty-four per cent of West Glamorgan's redundancies. In the latter half of 1980 and 1981 Port Talbot accounted for thirty per cent of the county's redundancies, but in the first eight months of 1982 this proportion had once more increased (to thirty-four per cent).

The redundancies which occurred up to June 1980 amounted to nearly forty per cent of the total number of jobs in Port Talbot in 1976. Something like half of these redundancies occurred at BSC, but employment fell throughout manufacturing and, especially, in the construction industry. Even if the BSC figures are excluded, over 2,500 redundancies took place in Port Talbot in four peak months between January 1980 and May 1982.

Port Talbot's decline continued even after the blood-letting of 1980. Jobs were shed in every industry and in every size of firm. To begin with the larger employers, BP announced 500 redundancies at its Baglan Bay chemical works in 1982 and employment there had fallen to less than a thousand by 1984. At the neighbouring Llandarcy refinery BP cut 300 jobs in 1983 and announced 750 redundancies, leaving a workforce of 300, in January 1985. The Borg Warner transmission factory in Port Talbot recruited 200 workers — many of them BSC redundants — in April 1981 but by November 1983 the workforce stood at 910 and a year later it was down to 690. Even the Driving and Vehicle Licensing Centre in Swansea reduced employment in 1984: DVLC had 2,000 fewer jobs than at the peak employment level of 6,000 and another 500 jobs were due to go by 1987. The Local Authority also reduced employment: Afan Borough Council dispensed with 200 full-time jobs between autumn 1983 and winter 1984 (when it employed 600 full-time workers)

In the wake of *large*-scale redundancies in *large* firms throughout Britain in the early 1980s, many people appeared to put their faith in the employment potential of the small-business sector. Interviews with half-a-dozen *medium-sized* firms in Port Talbot revealed that all had reduced employment by twenty-five per cent *or more* between 1980 and 1982. A survey of eighty-four *small* firms[3] in 1982 showed that one in four had announced redundancies or planned redundancies since 1980. Redundancies were, however, only one means of reducing employment. Service sector firms were particularly likely to reduce employment through 'natural wastage'. The service sector did not produce significant numbers of notifiable redundancies but (slow) growth in labour demand in this sector in the 1970s turned into decline all the same.

The small firms survey demonstrated that decline in the service sector had continued even when manufacturing job losses started to decelerate after the disastrous year of 1980. In *distribution* the retailers had fared much worse than wholesalers: some retailers had actually shut up shop (literally) between 1980 and 1982 and none had opened over this period. Some of the retailers who had remained in business had reduced employment. Employers in the remainder of the service sector (outside distribution) had severe difficulties in maintaining employment between 1980 and 1982. Although there were no closures, there was only one new business (in banking and finance) and there seemed to be little growth potential, either for existing firms or new ones, in 1982. This turned out to be something of an understatement. In the following year Port Talbot lost three supermarkets, a cinema, a tax office and a medical centre. This was the worst-ever year for business failures in Wales and a total of 455 companies went to the wall, an increase of forty-two per cent on the previous year (*South Wales Evening Post*, 5 November 1984). Retailers and firms in the motor industry, construction, and engineering were hardest hit. Port Talbot had its fair share of these failures, especially bankruptcies (*Port Talbot Guardian* 29 September 1983). In 1984 Port Talbot lost more of its local services: a nightclub, a bank and — at the cost of forty jobs — a hotel (the Grand); all 'failed in Wales'.

Some of the job losses outside steel can be blamed on the 'knock-on' effects of the BSC redundancies. The decline of disposable income in Port Talbot explains the closure of supermarkets, nightclubs and hotels. As one of the employers in the small firms survey explained:

> 'The recession is being felt by us as never before. The people in this area have little loose change in their pockets, no job prospects and young people have little hope. We will not give up without a fight but it will be hard going.'

But the 'knock-on' effects of the redundancies could not have produced more than a small percentage of the job losses outside steel. For one thing, Chapter Two showed that Port Talbot had never had much of a service sector to begin with. There simply weren't enough jobs to lose for service sector losses to make much of an impact. Furthermore, not all of the service sector jobs Port Talbot did have *could* be affected by any loss of purchasing power following the BSC redundancies. The (slow) growth areas of employment in the service sector in the 1970s had been education and health where jobs were dependent on government spending and not on incomes.

The 'knock-on' effect of the redundancies at BSC were limited because it was a manufacturing town. Local manufacturing either didn't depend on demand from BSC or that demand didn't fall (see Chapter Six). Nevertheless, being a manufacturing town didn't help Port Talbot. In part declining employment outside steel followed from this fact: it was simply an acceleration of the trend already described in Chapter Two. Port Talbot had too many jobs in those parts of manufacturing industry where employment across the whole country was declining. To some extent this was also true of Port Talbot's construction industry but here the main cause of falling employment was falling public spending. BSC's demand for construction work actually *increased* immediately after the redundancies[4] but job losses in construction continued. Chapter Two showed that construction had accounted for an abnormally high percentage of Port Talbot's jobs. Many of these jobs were funded by public spending on major projects like the redevelopment of the town centre and the new motorway. The supply of public money for these projects had dried up by 1980.

Economists would describe what happened to Port Talbot as 'deindustrialisation' but there are more elegant ways to describe the process. As the job losses gathered pace the graffiti on the Severn Bridge announced that 'Wales is Closed'. This was presumably written with the steel redundancies in mind and these did not affect the whole of Wales by any means. However, as the months passed the epitaph seemed more and more appropriate since the rest of Wales was soon reduced to the same condition as Port Talbot. Thus, for most of the period 1980/82 *all* areas in West Glamorgan had remarkably similar experiences of rising unemployment. Port Talbot's published unemployment rate was higher than the Welsh unemployment rate, but not by much. In the summer of 1981, however, the rate of unemployment in the Port Talbot 'travel-to-work area' (a somewhat larger area than the town itself) fell below West Glamorgan's unemployment rate and stayed below it until November 1982. (Unemployment in Port Talbot increased once more but the rate of increase was lower than in neighbouring areas in the latter half of 1981 and for most of 1982). Although Port Talbot was especially hard-hit in 1980, the rest of Wales soon caught up.

*New Jobs For Old?*
According to the 'deindustrialisation' theory, Wales used to produce things (for example steel) which people wanted, but by 1980 these things were no longer in demand. The producers (firms and workers) of these things were no longer needed and so Wales was closed. One difficulty with this theory is that it takes no account of government policy, something that was surely in the minds of the writers of the Severn Bridge epitaph. For decades, including decades of booming demand, Wales had required regional aid in order to generate anything like full employment.

An alternative, 'regional problems' theory would look something like this: some areas have not been able to generate sufficient employment and full employment in these areas was created by government intervention. When government help is withdrawn these areas revert to type and unemployment is created. In order to reduce unemployment, government will have to create jobs once more. How does this theory measure up to the facts?

Restrictions on public spending did Port Talbot a great deal of harm. Throughout the post-war period Britain's steel industry had been used as an instrument of regional policy[5] and governments had put steel plants where work was needed (Morgan, 1983). The choice of Port Talbot as a site for one of the large integrated plants reflected the underlying weakness of the local economy. This weakness was disguised until 1980 when the BSC redundancies were announced and the full extent of Port Talbot's plight was revealed.

Job losses in steel and construction can be blamed on reductions in public spending but it would be a mistake to think that Port Talbot received no government aid after 1980. Port Talbot still received government assistance — albeit at a reduced level — however, this 'help' took a different form. Before 1980 the game of public investment was played by different rules from those observed by private investors: public investment (in steel or roads for example) took account of the social consequences of investment decisions. After 1980 most government assistance to Port Talbot fell into one of two categories. Firstly, BSC received financial assistance which, while ensuring the plant's survival, actually brought about further job losses there (see Chapter Eight). Secondly, government money was made available as loans or subsidies to private firms without guarantees on the employers' part about the volume — or nature — of the employment they would create.

In fact private firms were reluctant to take advantage of government assistance with or without employment guarantees, as the local authority discovered. Between 1980 and 1983, 18,757 job losses (including redundancies) in the Port Talbot travel-to-work area had been reported in the press. Where would the employers who would replace these jobs be found? In times such as these people will cast around for any clue; and this was especially true of those officers and councillors charged with the government of the town. Their disorientation forced them to grasp at straws in the wind. In 1980 the wind blew few straws in the direction of Port Talbot, but when one did appear it was tightly grasped. Like many other local authorities throughout the UK, Afan Borough decided that new technology and the microprocessor could help them replace the jobs that had disappeared in industries which had provided employment for decades. They could not be sure what the future was going to look like, but perhaps it could be made in the image of the silicone chip.

Port Talbot did have one firm which suggested that this hi-tech version of the future might be possible. I shall call them 'Griffin'. Griffin made 30,000 cheap computers a month for the home-computer market. They were important to Port Talbot not simply because they represented the town's only stake in the hi-tech future, but also because of the kind of people they employed. Griffin became an independent public company in late 1982, just after establishing their first production line. They then employed thirty-six people. Three months later they moved from Swansea to an industrial estate on the outskirts of Port Talbot. They moved to Port Talbot to take advantage of government aid, including help with premises, made available through the Welsh Development Agency (WDA). I went to see them in September 1983, by which time they had an annual turnover of £15 million and employed 230 people. Just under half of these were manual workers; the rest were technicians, research and development staff, clerical workers and management. Of the manual workers, thirty eight were *temporary* employees, with contracts specifying a maximum of six months' work. In subsequent weeks a further eighty-six manual workers were hired on temporary contracts to cope with the expected Christmas sales boom. Most of the staff — manual and non-manual — were young (and the majority were women). In other words, Griffin employed proportionately more of one of the groups most severely affected by rising unemployment in the town. The manager I talked to was responsible for recruitment and said she was 'keen on school-leavers and the unemployed'.

This manager's interest in recruiting amongst the young unemployed was genuine, and extended even to those who had been out of work for many months. But she did require that new recruits should have made 'an effort' to find work. Two years ago she would have had to 'think hard' about taking anyone who had been out of work for more than three months but things had changed so much since then that she would only 'start worrying' about someone who had been unemployed for over a year. In this case she would ask the potential recruit what they had been doing:

'If they say they've been getting up at eleven and playing pool, then "No!" But if they say, "Well, here's a list of the firms I've applied to," then "Yes".'

She also liked them to be able to give her references, even from a YTS scheme or a holiday job, so that she could check up.

Yet the fact that Griffin were so 'keen on school-leavers and the unemployed' is itself a warning about the shape of the hi-tech future. Working for Griffin was not, in the main, 'working with computers'. Heaven knows what everybody else in Port Talbot thought it was like — perhaps like playing one of Griffin's computer games all day — but the manual workers at Griffin knew well enough that their work was simple, repetitive, light-assembly work. The firm bought pre-assembled boards from a local manufacturer. The 'direct operators' soldered up some connections, put the boards in cases (also bought in), then stuck on the keyboards. After this there was testing by technicians, then despatch. In principle the operation was no different from the assembly lines used for the production of electrical goods for decades, and it is not remotely like 'working with computers'[6]. Griffin did not require qualifications of any kind for their direct operators, merely an interest in 'working in a factory', a good personality (especially in view of the young workforce), the 'ability to learn' and good attendance records.

Of course the people who were lucky enough to get jobs with Griffin did not mind too much about the nature of their work. As the manager said, Griffin were 'inundated' with applications and *dare not* use their name when advertising jobs in the local press because they would never be able to process all the applications. Whatever else it might be, a job at Griffin looked like an investment in the future; computers were the new thing and a firm that made them had to be secure. So never mind that the wages were a little lower than those paid by other local firms offering similar kinds of job — for example in the local tobacco factory which employed mainly women manual workers on £92 per week. At Griffin, direct operators had an average of thirteen weeks' training during which time they earned £75 per week (if over eighteen). After training they earned £86 per week. There were no bonuses but a fair bit of overtime, especially in the lead up to Christmas. Indirect operators — supplying the lines — earned £90 per week.

Electrical goods assembly lines — whether for computers or TVs — are surprisingly unsophisticated. They require little capital investment and no hardware which is difficult to move. When I went to see Griffin they were already in financial trouble — even the Press had picked this much up — and so, in view of their potential mobility, I asked if it was likely that they would re-locate in another area in the next two years. I was told that this was unlikely: they had had a lot of publicity — 'a ray of hope in an area of mass unemployment' — and had taken a great deal of trouble in building up and training the staff. On top of this two of the four directors were 'local' and, all in all, Griffin had a strong commitment to the locality. Griffin computers are now produced in Spain.

At one time Griffin was said to be 'the fastest growing company in *Wales*', never mind Port Talbot, but its rise and fall was brief indeed, barely two years of hope. What went wrong? Well, in a way *nothing* went wrong; it was simply that local expectations of the new technology were too great. In any new market lots of companies will go under, after the initial boom, before the market stabilises. One city analyst described the personal computer industry in this way:

'It is now simply showing signs of being an immature industry. That means rationalisation, but the characteristics of the industry are basically healthy.' (Quoted in *Sunday Times*, 6 November 1983)

The 'shake-out' hit personal computer manufacturers in the United States first, just at about the same time as I was visiting Griffin. There were fears of a drop in prices similar to that which had affected the producers of pocket calculators (*Guardian*, 22 September 1983) and there were no longer rich pickings as the number of manufacturers increased. Together with increased competition, existing producers were running out of consumers: the market, especially in the UK, was reaching saturation point. Price-cutting for real came within a couple of months, just as IBM came into the market for (business) personal computers. By then the best-informed city analysts were sure that Griffin's remaining life was short; so was I. People with no direct interest in Griffin knew that the firm would not last long into the new year, yet the 230 employees, with everything depending on its fate, knew nothing. Griffin went into receivership at the end of May 1984; seventy one jobs were left in June. It was sold two months later: thirty five jobs were left in Port Talbot and 100 'new' jobs created in Spain.

So Griffin became one of the necessary casualties of a new industry; it just happened to be in Port Talbot. But this isn't quite right. That Griffin was in Port Talbot at all followed from the firm's twin handicaps: it was small and, relatedly, it needed financial help. These were the two reasons why Griffin did not survive whereas some of its competitors did. When the going got tough the bigger firms could squeeze out the competition because they could cope with temporary cash flow problems for longer. They had more reserves to draw on and didn't have to rely on finance from sales. They could afford to take losses for a while in order to run big advertising campaigns, buy up (through discounts) exclusive control of distribution networks, and develop new, more attractive products. Griffin's first model was soon out of date — it had a 'slow chip' — and the firm never managed to break into the more lucrative *business* computer market. But it was a cash flow crisis that eventually killed off Griffin, even if its competitors arranged the execution.

Griffin had had a lot of public money through the Welsh Development Agency (WDA). They had had help with premises and equipment and they needed this help because they were small. The 'price' they paid for assistance was locating in Port Talbot. But it was, in the end, private capital that pulled the plug on Griffin. The WDA owned 23 per cent of the firm, and another local company owned 15 per cent, but 42 per cent was in the hands of a major 'institutional' investor. This institution had already helped Griffin out in the summer of 1983 with a cash injection two or three times greater than the price eventually paid for Griffin's assets. The money was intended to help Griffin get over cash flow problems incurred in new product development. (In return for this help Griffin had to appoint a new managing director). When the financial crisis returned, the institutional investor was not prepared to throw good money after bad.

Compared to the other fruits of government assistance to Port Talbot after 1980, Griffin was something of a success story. Afan Borough Council, like its competitors elsewhere in the UK, was reduced to stealing jobs from its neighbours in an effort to share out the misery of unemployment more fairly. The trouble was, they weren't very good at it.

As part of their introduction to the subject, anthropology students are usually told of the existence of something called a 'cargo cult' on certain tropical islands. The natives of these islands are said to have watched White men arrive on aeroplanes and unload all the goodies of modern civilisation: tee-shirts, transistor radios and outboard motors. To the islanders these goodies literally came out of the sky and all that seemed to be necessary to ensure a continual supply was to make the planes arrive by building a sort of landing strip and sticking up a few totems such as hand-fashioned images of planes to advertise their existence. The islanders, students are told, then sat down at the end of their hand-made runway and waited.

There is good evidence to suggest that a cargo cult is alive and flourishing in Port Talbot. On a 176-acre site next to the motorway the WDA installed drains and roads and advanced factories. There were originally meant to be ninety of these but there were only *nine* when the estate opened. As we will see, things seem to have changed since the plans were first drawn up. Nevertheless, Port Talbot's Baglan Moors Industrial Estate is evidence of a cargo cult at the end of the M4 corridor, but the goodies get scarce after Swindon, or at least Bridgend. (Bridgend has a Sony factory, where a £36 million investment created sixty new jobs in 1983/4, and a Ford factory which was entirely built with public money and employed 1,800 people in 1984[7]). All the same, the natives believe that the vacant lots will bring them goodies; they have an unshakeable faith in their own version of cargo cult:

'I am convinced that future economic forces will shift the industrial centre of gravity of the United Kingdom westward towards South Wales — and Port Talbot will be ready.'(Mayor of Afan, Councillor Bill Harris,*Port Talbot Guardian*, 24 May 1984)

It might be said, with some justification, that this is all a little unfair. Port Talbot has really tried to increase local employment — 'Port Talbot means business' as the Council's slogan says — and it has a lot to offer. It was the only borough in South West Wales with Special Development Area status, and also had Inner Urban status which increased its chances of receiving Urban Aid funding through the Welsh Office. With Inner Urban status the Council was able to designate the old dockland as an industrial improvement area. In addition there were *ninety-five* different grants available to small firms. Afan had £½ million from the EEC in 1983/4 and £10 million from the WDA for the Baglan Moors estate. But the sad thing is, most of this money was thrown away. By November 1985, only one of the Baglan Moors factories had been occupied. Leaving aside the forgone rates (Afan offers new companies two rate-free years plus other incentives) and the cost of the land, once scheduled for houses and schools, this worked out at a cost of £2 million per job.

The Baglan Moors development was originally intended to cost £20 million. This money was supposed to create in excess of five *thousand* jobs. The Council has always complained that they were short-changed by the Government and the WDA but when the estate was officially opened with nine factories in November 1983 it was still without a single tenant. In the absence of a story the press reports of the opening took on the tone of farce. They described the cargo cult's totem:

'Baglan Industrial Park's estate sign is 96 feet long and 26 feet high — one of the largest signs of its type in South Wales.'

(*South Wales Evening Post*, 11 November 1983)

The survey of small firms in Port Talbot revealed that some employers blamed the *Government* for many of the cost increases which threatened their survival. They looked to the Government to hold down industrial rates for users of gas, electricity and telephones. Other respondents blamed the *local authority* for rising costs, especially in regard to rates (fifty per cent of Afan's rates income depended on BSC and BP Baglan Bay, *Port Talbot Guardian*, 22 February 1984), but respondents were also critical of policy — of government policy in general and of local authority policy. It is perhaps surprising how much criticism was directed at the local authority. It seems that whatever the Borough Council's success in attracting new business to the area, respondents felt that too little was being done to maintain employment in existing firms.

Many found the local authority unhelpful and in some cases local
authority policy was thought to be possibly harmful — for example,
redevelopment was thought to have harmed the trade of several
retailers. But the shopkeepers did seem to be pleased — even if the
general public was a little bemused — by the Council's latest effort:
in 1984 work began on a new £5 million town hall. Not that the
Council seems to have lost faith in its cargo cult, however. They
recently announced a £55,000 feasibility study into the possibility of
setting up a hovercraft base in Port Talbot. If the goodies won't
come from the motorway, perhaps they'll come from the sea!

In a town which seems to monopolise irony, it is quite apt that the
only hope for Port Talbot should come from an industry which
seemed to be in even bigger trouble than the one the town had relied
on for some years. There had been talk of a 'superpit' at Margam, to
the east of the steelworks, for many years. Despite an NCB
disclaimer in 1983, rumours circulated of their intention to invest
anything up to £400 million in Margam and of their plans to create
over a thousand new jobs. EEC cash was available to help and,
although the NUM warned that the NCB was stalling so that
Margam's coal reserves could be privatised and local residents
expressed doubts about damage to the environment, there was
much apparent enthusiasm. Finally, the NCB gave the go-ahead to
the development: not, however, for the deep pit which had been
intended, but for a drift mine costing £90 million and creating 700
mining jobs. The new pit would employ fewer people than the
doomed St John's pit only three miles away although it would, of
course, produce a lot more coal.

Government assistance has brought few jobs to Wales in the
1980s. Even at peak employment, the Ford factory at Bridgend
provided only a tenth of the jobs lost by that time in the Welsh steel
industry alone. As the example of Ford suggests, the jobs which
were created with government money have rarely lasted. Firms
have certainly moved to Wales, and new jobs have been created,
but the record of closures and bankruptcies, and of job losses, has
kept pace (see, for example, *South Wales Evening Post*, 29 June
1983). In large part it is the same set of firms in each set of figures
since new firms make up the list of casualties. Thus the survey of
small firms in Port Talbot revealed that some 'new' firms may in fact
have represented second or third attempts to establish a viable
business. In some cases there may not actually be room for new
entrants but conventional assessments of market potential may be
of little relevance given the importance of other factors, in
particular financial assistance to would-be entrants and their
employees. We should also note that such calculations are in any
case of little relevance in recession since at such times the rate of

business formation, *and failure*, generally rises because of the increase in the number of people — both potential employers and employees — for whom the only alternative to new business formation is the dole.

Where new jobs *have* lasted they have rarely been as well-paid as the jobs they were intended to replace. The few well-paid jobs that have been created have not, in the main, gone to local people. Between August 1982 and December 1983 113 factories opened in West Glamorgan. These new factories created 1,200 jobs but only 380 of them went to local people. The rest were taken by people who had moved into the area with their companies (*South Wales Evening Post* 5 January 1984). There is, however, one group of local workers who seemed to have got more than their fair share of any new jobs that were created (although not necessarily by new firms) — the workers made redundant by BSC[8].

*Unemployment*
Official unemployment in the Port Talbot 'travel-to-work area' reached a peak of 17.1 per cent (18 per cent for men and 15.5 per cent for women) in October 1982. In November of that year the method of counting the numbers of people out of work was changed and the unemployment rate for the area dropped. The Port Talbot travel-to-work area includes other towns — Bridgend and Maesteg — as well as smaller settlements, and gives only a very rough guide to unemployment in Port Talbot itself. Unfortunately, *rates* of unemployment are not calculated for individual Employment Office Areas (EOAs) and we must be content with numbers of men and women on the register. Male and female unemployment in the Port Talbot EOA was already rising before the spring of 1980; however in the summer of that year there was a sharp rise in numbers out of work. Unemployment amongst women increased by fifty per cent by October of that year while *male* unemployment more than doubled (according to a survey — see Chapter Four — of the BSC redundants, less than ten per cent of the redundants who were unemployed were women). In subsequent months unemployment continued to increase, although more gradually, and there was no significant decline until November 1982 when the Government's method of counting the unemployed changed[9]. By September 1982 total numbers out of work in the Port Talbot EOA had reached 228 per cent of the numbers in January 1980.

Much of the massive increase in unemployment in Port Talbot in 1980 can be explained by the BSC redundancies in that year. The bulk of these redundancies *occurred* in the latter half of the year (July being the peak month). The effect of these large flows onto the labour market is visible in the Job Centre's unofficial count of

numbers joining and leaving the register: the flow of people onto
the register was much greater in the first nine months of 1980 than in
any succeeding month. The size of these flows — relative to the
unemployed 'stock' — exceeds anything obtained under 'normal'
circumstances, even where large redundancies have occurred,
however not all of the workers joining the unemployment register
had been made redundant by BSC.[10] There were some — although
more in later years — who were casualties of the other redundancies
described earlier in this chapter, and there were others who were
'new entrants' to the labour market. Unemployment in the
'unclassified by industry' category increased by sixty per cent in
1980. This heading includes people without previous work
experience and about one in three of this group were school-
leavers[11].

   While an increase of one hundred per cent in male
unemployment in less than a year seems bad enough, we might have
expected something even more disastrous. There are several
reasons why the full effects of job losses in Port Talbot were not
reflected in the unemployment figures. Firstly, a high number of
jobs in the town had been held by people who were not residents.
BSC, in particular, drew its labour force from a much wider area
than that used to calculate the town's unemployment figures.
Residents of other areas were among those made redundant and the
effects of job losses in the town were felt in all the neighbouring
areas which sent workers to Port Talbot. While travel-to-work
patterns ensured that some of Port Talbot's unemployment was
exported to other areas, commuting patterns *also* ensured that not
all of the towns' residents were employed in the town's (vulnerable)
industries. Some of these residents — especially women working in
the service sector — had jobs outside the town with firms which did
not reduce employment at the same rate as the (manufacturing)
firms concentrated in Port Talbot.

   Secondly, there was a decline in the 'economically active'
population of Port Talbot[12]. Much of this decline was due to the fact
that some BSC redundants 'withdrew' from the labour market.
Only two-thirds of the redundants who lived in Port Talbot
registered as unemployed. Many of the 'missing' redundants were
older workers who withdrew from the labour market altogether.
Thirdly, some of the redundants found places on retraining schemes
after redundancy[13].

   Finally, some of the people who joined the unemployment
register found work. The rate of increase in Port Talbot's
unemployment slowed after 1980 and this had a lot to do with the
fact that many of the workers made redundant by BSC had left the
register: unemployment in the category 'metal manufacture' began

to fall soon after the redundants became unemployed. This compensated, at least in part, the continuing flow of workers from other industries, and of new entrants to the labour market, onto the register. Not all of the redundants who ceased to be counted as unemployed defined themselves as 'retired' or underwent retraining. Some found work.

The official figures do not suggest that the ex-steelworkers found jobs in steel. In part this was because some of them found work in other industries. (Because the supply of work in these other industries was not increasing, steelworkers displaced other groups of workers: the unemployment created by the redundancies at BSC was 'displaced' onto these other groups). Nevertheless, some *did* find work in steel. The official figures do not reveal this fact because the private contractors who supplied the jobs were not counted as part of the iron and steel industry. The creation of 'new' jobs with the contractors helps to explain why flows *off* the unemployment register were at their highest when flows *onto* the register reached their peak. The pattern of job loss *and* creation had the same cause: the Slimline Agreement and its after-effects. The labour market in Port Talbot was not static (as we might have expected). Flows *off* the register increased substantially in 1980 and Port Talbot's labour market revealed an unexpected dynamism. This dynamism reflected, for the most part, the fact that a reduction in voluntary job-changing was counter-balanced by an increase in activity amongst workers who were *compelled* to change their jobs.

Despite rising unemployment and despite all the evidence of job losses in this chapter, neither the 'deindustrialisation' nor the 'regional problems' theories provide a satisfactory explanation of what happened in Port Talbot (or the rest of Wales). One theory assumes that Wales was closed as a result of changes in demand: the other that Wales was closed by the Government. In fact both are wrong since Wales was not closed, as the redundant steelworkers who found work after leaving BSC discovered. Their experience, together with the dynamism of the Port Talbot labour market, shows that what happened was more complex: there was a change in the *form*, and not simply the *volume*, of work in Welsh industry.

**Footnotes**
1. I am indebted to both Huw Beynon and Chris Harris for this insight.
2. For further details see Fevre, 1984a.
3. For further details see Fevre, 1984b.
4. BSC's demand for construction work fell in 1982 when the 'Concast' project was completed but rose again for a period between 1984 and 1986 when the hot strip mill was refurbished. Further details of both of these projects are given in Chapter Eight.

5.  Even before the war new steelworks provided employment for workers displaced from other jobs, however it was not considered necessary to site the works in the area where jobs were needed. The steelworks at Corby, in the English Midlands, drew *its* workforce from the West of Scotland.

6.  Compare to the description of work in a television factory given in Fevre, 1981.

7.  Ford in Bridgend recruited some of the workers made redundant by BSC but also had to absorb over 300 workers from the Ford plant at Swansea.

8.  The jobs that they found would not necessarily appear in any official figures since they were *temporary* and, on occasion, 'off the books' (see Chapter Five).

9.  The method used to calculate the numbers of unemployed was changed on several occasions. However, the November 1982 change (which removed those not claiming benefit from the figures) had the greatest effect on the official count.

10. For further information on the composition of unemployment in Port Talbot see Fevre 1984a.

11. There was no improvement in the employment prospects of school-leavers in subsequent years. Out of a total of 200 fifth-form leavers at a Port Talbot comprehensive school in 1984, only *seven* found full-time employment (*Port Talbot Guardian*, 19 April 1984).

12. This was due to two causes: a small drop in population and a drop in the proportion of the population who were in work or *available* for work. Either change may represent *hidden* unemployment. Thus workers may leave the area because they lose their jobs (this was undoubtedly the case with some construction workers and helps to explain why Port Talbot's unemployment remained low despite job losses in construction in the 1970s) or they may decide there is no point in being available for work because no work is available for them.

13. For further information on the fate of the redundant steelworkers see Harris *et al* (forthcoming).

Chapter Four

# Tender Invitations

*Slimline and the Contractors*

Pieces of this complicated story are now beginning to come together, just as they did when the research was under way. We now know that there were some new jobs in Port Talbot after 1980 and we know that some of those made redundant by BSC found work. Just about the time the connection between these two pieces of information became clear, I had begun to ask current BSC employees what had been happening in the steelworks since the redundancies in 1980. I was interested in the reorganisation that had allowed such a substantial fall in employment (in excess of the reduction in output at BSC) and I wanted to know how rising unemployment had affected the attitudes of those workers who remained. It did not take long, in any of my conversations with these workers, for them to mention the increased use of contractors by BSC.

Using a variety of sources, we can build up a picture of how the increased use of contractors came about. It was probably considered by the BSC Board between October and November 1979; at any rate, the document *Return to Financial Viability*, dated 10th December 1979, mentioned contracting in general terms as a possible method of achieving job losses throughout BSC. But what of BSC Port Talbot? Chapter Two referred to secret talks in progress at Port Talbot in December 1979.

At this time the Director of BSC Port Talbot and the works management committee told union officials at the plant which departments and jobs were going to be cut. The union officials were also told *how* the cuts were to be brought about in each case. Management told them, in each case, whether jobs would disappear because of (a) reduced output (b) changes in working practices, or (c) the increased use of outside contractors. In February 1980 these three methods of bringing about reductions in employment were enshrined in the argument for Slimline presented to the BSC Board by the Chief Executive. *Return to Financial Viability: Presentation of South Wales Options*, (BSC 1980) demanded 'the freer use of contractors where operationally and financially desirable.'

On the 3rd of April the national steel strike ended and local officials set about selling Slimline to the workforce following the return to work. During this time many workers were told that if they

accepted the redundancies they would get jobs with the contractors.
Meanwhile negotiations between BSC and the prospective
contractors began, and some senior trade union sources believe that
initial talks were held even before the end of the strike in April.
Slimline was signed on 15th May 1980 and thereafter many
employees considering voluntary redundancy were advised by their
shop stewards, as well as by the 'counsellors' employed by BSC,
that they could expect to find work with contractors back at BSC
after redundancy.

The increased use of contractors was described as one of the
'major areas' of the Slimline agreement, and the Slimline document
included the following references to contractors:

> 'The use of Contractors on a regular basis on the following work and
> duties is agreed:-
>
> i    Maintenance/Repairs inclusive of Civil Engineering Bricklayers
> ii   Mobile Plant
> iii  Internal Road Transport
> iv   Slag Tipping
> v    Scrap Handling/Preparation
> vi   Catering
> vii  Amenities
> viii General Housekeeping and Plant Cleaning
> ix   Technical Publications
> x    Project Engineering.'

In fact, we will see below that not all of these ten areas were put
out to tender. Catering, for example, remained a BSC operation
after some difficulties in negotiations with the prospective
contractor. Some additional areas of work not listed here *were* put
out to contract, however. As the Slimline document made clear,
this was entirely within the terms of the agreement:

> 'The management reserve the right to use contractors on other work as
> necessary ...'.

Although it was added that 'Such contract work will be confined
to peak workloads', Appendix Two of the document stated that one
of the 'principles/working practices' to be introduced immediately
was 'No restriction on the use of Contractors within or *ex* works'.[1]

At the neighbouring Llanwern steelworks in Newport the
equivalent (Slimline) agreement, also signed in 1980, included an
Appendix listing 'committed principles for determining manning
levels':

> 'The manpower reductions for "Slimline" are carried primarily by the
> change in plant configuration and shift patterns, but a significant
> number relate to the necessary introduction of internationally

competitive working practices and principles. It is agreed that the workforce which remains must adopt these new practices and principles in order to sustain operations at maximum efficiency.

'In total, the basis for "Slimline" manning depends upon the following committed principles ...

'3. Complete cessation *by direct sources* of some functions and services, e.g. Catering, Industrial Engineering, O & M, the Drawing Office facility is severely curtailed.' (Emphasis added)

Elsewhere in the Llanwern document it was stated that contractors would be invited to tender for mobile plant, painting and decorating, overall service and janitors/general cleaners in 1981. The possibility of replacing the Central Engineering Workshop (including electrical services) by contractors was also raised. One of the 'Committed Principles' of the Llanwern agreement was that:

'Contractors will continue to be used for peak maintenance, capital and specialist work.'

Both agreements, Port Talbot's as well as Llanwern's, specified areas of work which went out to tender for the first time ever in 1980 or 1981, but some of the principles (regarding the use of contractors) which they contained *appeared* to have been working in practice, although not formally agreed, for many years. BSC policy on the use of contractors was stated in 1969:

'It is the Corporation's policy that wherever possible its own employees should do all the necessary work in the Corporation. However, there will be occasions such as emergencies, peak loads and unattractive or highly specialised work where the Corporation will need to supplement its own labour force by the use of contractors. These occasions will be kept to a minimum.'

The trade unions did not formally agree this policy statement but were nonetheless a lot happier, in retrospect, with BSC's statement 'that wherever possible its own employees should do all the necessary work' than they were with the Port Talbot Slimline document which told them BSC would accept 'no restriction on the use of Contractors'. It is clear that the Slimline agreements at Port Talbot and elsewhere did not merely formalise established practices, but signalled a completely new departure in the use of contractors by BSC.

The 1969 policy statement listed several areas of work (excluding 'major capital developments') where contractors had been used in some way in a BSC establishment:

'(a) Development work in or alongside existing plant.
(b) The use of contractors in certain defined work, e.g. window

cleaning, painting, slag handling, scrap recovery, internal road traffic.

(c) Use of contractors to supplement the existing workforce, e.g. bricklaying, furnace wrecking.

(d) Use of contractors during stop weeks.

(e) Any highly specialised work.'

BSC Port Talbot had, at some time, used contractors for work under all of these headings before 1980. It may be more useful, however, to categorise pre-1980 contracting work at Port Talbot according to the various 'reasons' for putting the work out to contract.

Firstly, the *inflexibility* of the BSC workforce was mentioned by both workers and managers. For example, strict demarcation between crafts in planned (regular) maintenance left gaps which contractors were able to fill. Inflexibility also created problems where BSC workers had to cope with peaks in demand, and this problem occurred in occasional (for instance, breakdown) maintenance as well as in planned maintenance. In theory BSC's maintenance team could be drafted in wherever their work was needed, but in practice each department had its own team and contractors were needed to make up the numbers where a large input of labour was required for a short period.

Secondly, contractors were brought in to do jobs which, for one reason or another, BSC employees *did not want to do*. For example, BSC's steel erectors might think a particular job was too dirty or too wet; or BSC's labourers would refuse the dirty and hazardous work of cleaning up acid on the pickling line. Similar circumstances probably accounted for the intrusion of contracting into slag handling (including extraction of iron from slag).

Thirdly, contractors were used where there simply *weren't enough workers* on the BSC payroll to do the work. Thus contractors were used to supplement the BSC workforce for large installation jobs and for construction, engineering and civil engineering projects. Similarly, some occasional maintenance tasks which had to be undertaken in a workshop were given to off-site contractors when BSC's own Central Engineering Shop was overloaded. In fact, in the 1970s BSC were under increasing pressure to bring more contractors into occasional and planned maintenance (on site) as the amount of maintenance required increased. One of the people responsible for the implementation of BSC's planned maintenance policy explained that when it began after the first few years of operation in the 1950s, planned maintenance was intended to eliminate the possibility of breakdowns which resulted from wear and tear. It was also originally intended to eliminate the possibility of breakdowns caused by design weaknesses and, from the beginning, BSC's engineers were told that the plant had to be 'self-sufficient' in maintenance terms. For example, the engineers were required to get hold of all the plans of new equipment installed in the works from the manufacturers (an often difficult task). Yet as time went on, the preventive aspects of maintenance became more and more demanding. As the plant aged the workers found they could no longer complete all the maintenance required when the plant was stopped for that purpose and breakdowns began to occur with increasing frequency (especially in the rolling mill) in the 1970s.

Finally, tenders were invited for *specialist* work. This is clearly the reason for using contractors for occasional maintenance where the contractor manufactured or installed the equipment being maintained; however, some regular maintenance was also put in this category and here the work may have overlapped with that described in one or other of the three categories already discussed. For example, a job might be described as specialist simply because BSC's own workforce were reluctant to do it.

The possibility of using contractors on a very large scale had been present in BSC's thinking for two decades. In the 1960s steel executives began to visit Japan to observe, and approve, the extensive use of contractors in Japanese steelworks. BSC were no doubt impressed by the level of contracting out in their supposedly more efficient competitors: other steel producers, even some European plants, had more contract workers than direct employees. Nevertheless, even in the period immediately preceding the announcement of the redundancies in 1980, BSC appeared to be treating the contracting option with caution (Hicks, 1980). It was not yet agreed that the 'Japanese' solution could successfully be applied in the UK.[2]

The possibility of extending the area of a steel plant which might be covered by outside contractors was obvious on those envy-ridden missions to (first) Europe and (then) Japan. But, unlike the idea of concentrating steelmaking on large coastal sites, for example, the increased use of contractors never became part of *the* plan for the development of British steel production. This did not, of course, mean that BSC did not use outside contractors. Contractors *were* used, but not for the most important activity of BSC, making steel. Whereas the Japanese couldn't seem to see why an electrician or a driver should be a steelworker or, for that matter, why workers in these categories should be on site all the time, 'steelmaking' in the UK might be interpreted to mean almost everything, from building the plant to delivering the steel. Even in early 1979, then, contractors remained 'just an option'. Indeed, at this time there were growing pressures on BSC to *reduce* their use of contractors.

Several contracting firms complained (and this was confirmed by management and trade union sources) that BSC's demand for contractors to do occasional or planned maintenance work had fallen because of falling output — there was now less plant to maintain and less wear and tear on remaining plant and equipment because it was working under capacity — and because BSC had simply ceased to bother about repair and maintenance. As proof of this change in BSC policy, contractors cited the increasing proportion of maintenance work which was being transferred from a planned maintenance schedule (with regular attention every week, for example) to an occasional maintenance basis (where work was only undertaken in the event of a breakdown). With Slimline, BSC gave up any remaining pretence that repair and maintenance was concerned with anything more than 'patching up'.

Finally, pressure to reduce the amount of work going out to contractors followed from changes which no longer gave BSC the same 'reasons' to put work out to contract. Slimline demanded complete flexibility of the BSC workforce; there were, for example, to be no demarcations between the various groups of craftsmen. Furthermore, even before the Slimline Agreement, the number of jobs which BSC workers did not want to do was falling. Thus at one time the Central Engineering Shop workforce — together with other groups of workers, for example those doing structural work — had *refused* work offered to them by management. But by the mid-1970s the threat of redundancies led to pressure from the workforce, through the trade unions, for the management to allow their own departments to compete with outside contractors for tenders that had usually gone outside the works as a matter of course. BSC workers were therefore given first option on these jobs and sometimes won the contract even if theirs was not the cheapest tender. As one of those involved remarked, there was 'manipulation'. Engineers in the departments concerned now had to secure the agreement of the shop stewards before inviting any tenders from outside contractors.

In spite of all these tendencies towards a *reduction* in the amount of work traditionally performed by contractors, there was, nevertheless, an increase in the amount of work contracted out by BSC. In 1980 and in subsequent years following Slimline and later agreements, however, the areas where contractors were now needed were not the same as before. Where contractors had *supplemented* BSC labour — on new installations and on maintenance for example — they now performed all or nearly all of the work; but contractors were also brought into *entirely new* areas, including what one union official called 'traditional steelworkers' jobs'.

*Contractors after Slimline*

The most visible effect of the change in use of contractors, at least for the steelworkers themselves, was an increase in the number of contractors' employees on site. Before 1980 there had been only a small number of regular maintenance contracting workers plus the contracting workers handling slag[3]; there were now far more contractors' employees in the works continuously. There were also far more contractors' employees on site on an irregular basis, for example during 'stop weeks'. All of the steel towns — whether Rotherham or Sheffield, Newport or Port Talbot — were long familiar with the annual shutdowns of their steelworks when contracting workers and even students doing summer jobs were drafted in to do repair and maintenance work alongside BSC maintenance staff. But it is a measure of the change in 1980 that one of the workers involved in 'stop fortnights' at Port Talbot for many years reckoned that in 1981 there were three times as many contractors' employees involved as there were before Slimline. These additional workers were doing the work of the BSC people who had been made redundant (see below).

Additional increases in work for contractors occurred in each of the subsequent years following Slimline in 1980. In 1981, for example, unions and management at Port Talbot signed the 'Survival I' agreement which reduced 'authorised manning' from the Slimline figure of 5,701 to 5,560. Appendix Eight of the document stated that reasons for the use of contractors might now include:

'(a) specialist skills not readily available
(b) non-availability of Works' direct labour on normal hours
(c) availability of contractors' labour on normal hours
(d) uneconomic use of direct labour.'

The document also repeated, as if this were really necessary, that there were to be 'no restrictions in the use of contractors within or ex-Works'.

The effect of Survival I, and of other agreements negotiated after 1980, was to extend the use of contractors in areas where contracting had already been introduced after Slimline , but also to introduce contractors into entirely new areas (with associated redundancies), for example, in the *Concast* department. The existing areas of contracting work which were affected were transport (including external transport), planned maintenance and new projects (for example, building Concast). Where there were no major projects under way, the number of (on-site) contracting workers involved in new project work seems to have been about the same as in the late 1970s, for example, about 250 contracting workers in mechanical engineering. For most of the period following Slimline BSC were involved in major new projects: first Concast and a new power plant, later the modernisation of the hot strip mill. Although there had been major projects in earlier years (the sinter plant, coke ovens and materials handling, for example), the contractors' input into, for instance, the Concast development was proportionally much greater. There were no longer numbers of BSC employees, from the 'taskforce' for instance (these workers also dealt with peak maintenance demand), to help out. In 1984 the contracting employers' organisations expected their members' role in major projects to expand still further in the future.

In planned maintenance further (post-1980) increases in the use of contractors took the form of both an increase in the number of contracting workers on site continuously — thus contractors were brought into crane maintenance, for example as greasers, in the slabbing mill and the BOS plant in 1983 — and an increase in the number of contracting employees on site for the regular 'down-shifts'. Thus one of the contracting workers on the down-shift in the hot mill, which took place once every two weeks, estimated that contracting workers outnumbered BSC employees here by five to one by 1984. The original intention, at the time of Slimline, was for maintenance staff from other departments to be more mobile and to cover peaks of work like the hot mill down-shift. In part — as the Survival I document suggested — the increase in contracting work followed a reduction in the amount of overtime offered to BSC workers, but there had also been further (BSC) redundancies, including maintenance staff and workers in the BOS and Concast areas.

It is difficult to get hold of accurate figures for contracting workers. BSC do not officially release such figures and both individual trade unions and the TUC Economic and Steel Committees have complained about the lack of data from BSC. As one of the committees explained, in 1984, 'such information is not available these days from BSC headquarters'. In order to reach a reliable estimate of the numbers involved, we should deal first with new capital projects, where BSC's demand for contractors lasts only so long as the project is underway. At peak employment, over 500 contracting workers were used on the installation of Concast and the new power plant (completed in 1982). The next peak was reached during the refurbishment of the hot strip mill. According to management, about 2,500 contracting workers were at work on the strip mill refurbishment and on other capital projects in September 1985 (this work was completed in the following year).

Although it did not vary to anything like the extent of demand for contractors on capital projects, BSC's demand for other sorts of contracting work also fluctuated. According to management, a maximum of 300 contracting workers were employed on maintenance. However, this figure increased to over 500 during a 'stop week'. In addition to the maintenance workers there were also lorry drivers, cleaners and so on. I am not allowed to quote the figure put on the total number of contracting workers outside new capital projects (but including maintenance) by BSC Port Talbot. However, I am allowed to say that the total is 'in four figures, it's substantial — we've put a lot out to contractors, Oh, enormous amounts'. From other sources I would estimate a total of 2,000 contracting workers (excluding those on capital projects) in 1985. BSC Port Talbot's workforce had dropped to 4,746 by this time (table 2.1) and so there were rather more than two contracting workers for every five BSC employees. If workers on capital projects are included, the contracting workforce and BSC workforce can be seen to be roughly equal.

By the end of 1980 Port Talbot was much more advanced in putting work out to tender than the other large South Wales works, Llanwern, but proportionally more of the increase in contracting at Llanwern occurred in subsequent years. This more gradual process had been outlined in the Llanwern Slimline agreement, but in fact contracting out took longer than intended in some cases. Thus Llanwern's mobile plant department was not put out to contract until long after the date (in 1981) specified in the Slimline agreement. There were, however, other extensions of contracting which had not been specified in the 1980 agreement: one employers' organisation reported a substantial increase in work for contractors in mechanical engineering. In 1985 trade union officers responsible for Llanwern estimated a maximum of 1,000 contractors' employees on site, excluding workers on new capital projects, an increase of 800 from 1979. If these figures were reasonably accurate then the ratio of contracting workers to BSC workers at Llanwern had risen from 1:40 to 1:4, but union officials at Llanwern did not think the rise in the contractors' proportion of all workers had been quite as great at this. Union members of the plant's Works Committee estimated that between 500 and 600 employees of contractors, *including* workers on new capital projects but *excluding* areas such as slag reclamation where contractors were used before 1980, were on the site at any one time.

The pattern in the rest of South Wales was similar to the pattern at Llanwern. Thus one trade union officer wrote in 1983 that, throughout South Wales, the tide of contractors was continually advancing 'into production, maintenance and other areas'. He added that this was usually accompanied by redundancies of directly employed workers. Sources in the ISTC considered that contracting had gone just about as far as it could in South Wales by 1984, but added that Llanwern and Port Talbot had provided 'models' for other plants which were only now catching up.

The Llanwern Works Committee members claimed that they had proportionally fewer contractors than other BSC plants. They thought that South Yorkshire had been badly affected. This much is certainly true: the TUC Steel Committee was told, for example, that up to 400 jobs of the 1,500 being declared redundant in the Appleby Frodingham slimdown would be taken over by contractors. Indeed, it may be that the Scunthorpe works of BSC had as many contracting workers as Port Talbot, and the TUC Steel Committee heard from the South Yorkshire area of one trade union of

'the increasing number of contractors entering into the industry, particularly to cover jobs which for decades have been done by our own workforce. Accepting that there are always jobs for specialised contractors, it is quite a different matter for jobs like the following to be given out to contractors, i.e. office cleaners, janitors, platelayers, mobile equipment, welfare attendants and general labouring departments'.

The TUC Steel Committee also expressed concern about the increased use of contractors at BSC Ravenscraig in Scotland, and on Teesside BSC negotiated an agreement which permitted, for example, the use of contractors in emergency situations, down days, extended repair periods, specialised work, construction or installation of new plant, off-site work and replacement or supplementing of direct labour in certain services.

A union official from Teesside wrote, in 1984, that 'BSC are by no means finished in their efforts to make most service jobs contract.' This comment seemed to summarise the national situation as well. In January 1984 the TUC Steel Committee thought BSC had taken the extension of contracting work 'a very long way already, and are continuing to extend'. In April the Committee concluded that 'Contractors are now widely used throughout BSC, to an extent which was not even contemplated in the 1970s'.

*Contractors and the Redundancies.*
It is clear that much of the extension of contracting described by the TUC Steel Committee was bought at the cost of redundancies for BSC workers: Slimline and its successors at Port Talbot increased the use of contractors and put BSC employees out of work. It is, however, very difficult to estimate exactly how many of these redundancies resulted from the increased use of contractors. Nevertheless, we can get some idea of the level of job losses

involved in those sections and departments where contractors were brought into BSC Port Talbot as a result of Slimline. According to BSC's figures the Central Engineering Shop workforce *was cut in half*. Employment in other relevant departments — mobile plant (including plant and vehicle workshop and locomotive repair shop), engineering services and transport — was reduced by *more than 60 per cent*, and the refractories engineering workforce was cut by 41 per cent. Taken together, these five departments produced 1,783 redundancies in 1980. Of course not all of these redundancies resulted from the increased use of contractors but then 1,783 is not the total of redundancies in departments where work was put out to contract. Slimline brought contracting workers, albeit on a smaller scale, into other departments as well. In all, nearly half of the net job losses produced by Slimline were in departments which were to be affected by contracting[4]: 654 in maintenance in coke and iron, steel and slab, hot rolled products and cold rolled products; 1,331 in engineering services; 360 in other services; 92 in technical and major developments.

The management of BSC Port Talbot claim that 'one thousand jobs went (under Slimline) which were replaced by contractor services' but this estimate seems a little on the low side. In any event, it is certain that the proportion of job losses which resulted from the increased use of contractors rose in later years. Later job losses represented desperate attempts to reduce employment where all other avenues for job-cutting, for example increased flexibility of remaining staff, had been exhausted. The one remaining solution was to put the work out to tender. According to management, between 1,000 and 2,000 of the 7,000 jobs lost between 1979 and 1983 were replaced by contractors in or ex works.

With so much detailed information the reader could now be forgiven if s/he felt a little confused about exactly which areas of work BSC have put out to contract, and it would be wise to take stock at this point. We have seen that the Slimline agreement introduced contractors into maintenance/repairs, mobile plant, internal road transport, slag tipping, scrap handling/ preparation, amenities, general housekeeping and plant cleaning, and project engineering at BSC Port Talbot. Furthermore, we know that Slimline gave BSC a free hand in their use of contractors and that contracting workers were moved into additional areas after 1980.

What sort of occupations were involved in the contracting work created at BSC Port Talbot in 1980 and in subsequent years? In addition to various forms of labouring, there was a whole range of craft occupations and their auxiliaries (including mates): fitters and welders, riggers and steel erectors, boilermakers, electricians, roll-grinders and turners, painters, HGV drivers, fabricators, platers.

These craftsmen and labourers were employed in a variety of tasks throughout the works. The term 'craftsmen' is used intentionally: the vast majority of contracting workers at Port Talbot were men. The only significant group of female contracting workers were cleaners, and their numbers had dropped below 50 by 1984. (While women were a minority in the Port Talbot contractors' workforce, they made up a much larger proportion in some other BSC plants — see below — and made up the *majority* of contracting workers in privatised service industries. *Guardian*, 21st January, 1987)

Before giving some examples of the kind of work done by the contractors, readers might appreciate a brief description of the major processes undertaken in the Port Talbot steelworks.

*COKE AND IRON*

| COKE OVENS AND SINTER PLANT | $\longrightarrow$ | BLAST FURNACES |
|---|---|---|

$\downarrow$

*STEEL AND SLAB*

| BOS PLANT | $\longrightarrow$ | CONCAST OR SLABBING MILL ETC. |
|---|---|---|

$\downarrow$

*STRIP MILLS*

| *HOT ROLLED PRODUCTS* | *COLD ROLLED PRODUCTS* |
|---|---|

As this (very) simple flow chart shows, making steel strip is a three-stage process. *Firstly*, coke is produced from coal in the coke ovens and iron ore is treated in the sinter plant. They are then used to produce iron in the blast furnaces. *Secondly*, iron is combined with scrap and other materials to produce steel. This is done in the BOS plant. BOS stands for 'Basic Oxygen Steel'. When the steel is made it is very hot and liquid. To turn this steel into something (a slab for example) which could be rolled as strip used to be a complex process which first involved the production of ingots in the slabbing mill. But from 1982 Port Talbot also had Concast, the 'continuous casting' process which turns liquid steel into something (slab) that can be rolled in one stage. *Thirdly*, thick slabs of steel are rolled into longer, wider and thinner steel strip. Strip can be rolled when it is hot or when it is cold and so there is a hot strip mill and a cold strip mill. The cold strip mills are actually used for *finishing* and include the pickling and galvanising processes.

In *coke and iron* production contractors employed fitters and welders, mates and labourers for all sorts of maintenance work, for example, pipework, including work on breakdowns but also on major refurbishment work. A blast furnace refurbishment could be a three-month contract or much longer. It also gave jobs to contractors undertaking refractory work on the lining of the furnace and to steel erectors and scaffolders. In fact contractors in coke and iron might undertake a variety of jobs: glazing, carpentry and joinery, demolition work.

In *steel and slab* production contracting fitters and the rest were involved in regular and breakdown maintenance in the slabbing mill, soaking pits, BOS plant and Concast. Small numbers of them were on site continuously, for example working on the cooling rings in the BOS plant and in the soaking pits, and in crane maintenance. Contractors' labourers were continuously at work in the BOS plant and with scrap and slag handling associated with BOS, Concast and the slabbing mill. Other groups of workers were involved in roofing, painting, coke moving, lancing and burning.

In *hot rolled products*, contracting workers were involved in all the categories of maintenance work, especially on the fortnightly 'down-shift' in the hot mill itself and at the annual 'stop fortnight'. Contractors' craftsmen also installed and replaced equipment — pipes, cables and so on — as part of unplanned maintenance throughout the hot mill (as they did in the slabbing mill and the cold mill). Down-shifts and shutdowns also provided plenty of work for contractors' labourers who undertook heavy cleaning (this went on at a lower level all the time). In addition, there were similar one-off jobs for painters, roofers and so on as in coke and iron, steel and slab. In *cold rolled products* contracting workers were employed on similar tasks to their co-workers in hot rolled products. Some, for example fitters, were continuously at work on maintenance (including cranes and hydraulics) while there were also contracting workers continually at work in the annealing bay and in packaging and dispatch and in stocking.

This is far from an exhaustive list of contractors' jobs at BSC Port Talbot. Most of the jobs mentioned here were engineering or electrical. These fell into the category of, firstly, regular and continuous jobs such as repair and maintenance of cranes, hydraulics, heating and ventilating; but one must add to these the repair and maintenance of plant-wide services such as mobile plant and transport. Secondly, there were irregular jobs: break-down repairs, replacing worn-out equipment, installing new equipment (for example pipes, ducts or cables). Finally, there were planned (regular but not continuous jobs): replacing worn-out equipment, regular 'down-shifts' and 'stop weeks', regular refurbishments (for example of blast furnaces).

To engineering and electrical tasks must be added those which were close to *production* jobs in steel and slab and the mills, together with work on new projects and some plant-wide services not yet covered. Regular and continuous work in the latter included cleaning, mobile plant and transport operation, maintenance of structures, civil engineering, and amenities. Irregular work might also be cleaning (for example cleaning up materials spillage), maintenance of structures or civil engineering; and all of these types of work were also performed on a planned basis, for example cleaning on 'down-shifts' or at 'stop weeks'. To summarise all of this in the most simple way: contracting workers at Port Talbot provided services (including electrical and engineering services) on a regular, irregular and planned basis; work for capital projects on an irregular basis; and production work on a regular basis.

Although Llanwern was a similar plant to Port Talbot, the pattern of contracting work there differed in some respects. The Llanwern Slimline agreement earmarked a smaller number of areas for contracting, and catering was put out to contract at Llanwern whereas this was not the case at BSC Port Talbot. In some cases, however, the pattern was the same. Thus in 1984 Llanwern had nearly 300 contractors' employees working on mobile plant (including cranes) and cleaning gangs. They also had contractors in repair and maintenance, stores and administration, and new project work. Refurbishing work had also been put out to tender, although BSC retained a small gang to assist the contractors. At the smaller BSC works in South Wales there were contracting workers in cleaning, catering, amenities and specialist (craft) work. In addition, one small works at Landore (Swansea) had contractors' employees in assembly work. These workers were brought in in 1982 and by 1984 there were more contracting workers at Landore than BSC employees.

Much of this information on contracting work in BSC outside Port Talbot was gathered with the help of ISTC (at the national *and* local level). ISTC sources were also able to provide some information on contracting work in BSC outside South Wales. For example at Ravenscraig contractors were used in canteen and amenity-block services. Contracting workers were also at work as platelayers; and in the cutting-out squad, slab-dressing, vessel-blocking, greasing and in the coal-handling plant. Elsewhere in Scotland there were contracting workers employed as amenity attendants and in greasing, canteens and offices. At the Dalzell works contractors' employees were used for non-specialist labouring work, for example cleaning up waste, in the mills.

On Teesside there were contracting workers in the BOS, Concast and mills areas. They included fitters, welders, riggers, electricians and mill operators. There were also contracting workers employed as amenity attendants and as *labourers*. One union official at Lackenby claimed that

> 'The majority of all labouring work on site at Lackenby is done by contractors, on the BOS Concast area it is 100% contract labour, in the coil plate mill at least 50%, in the beam mill at least 70%, all site work i.e. the drains, roads, civil engineering (digging holes), refuse collection and good housekeeping is done by contract labour. They also do 60-70% of plate laying, all office cleaning ... On a smaller scale contractors have moved into lubrication on the mills and the whole of the oil stores system is out to contractors. Road haulage is another field where BSC personnel have lost out to contractors.'

The official emphasised that this was *not* an exhaustive list of work performed by contracting workers at Lackenby. Elsewhere in the north of England, all the smaller works had contractors' employees working as amenity attendants. Some had contractors in office cleaning, catering and platelaying; some had contractors in their mills, site services, pump houses. Others had contracting workers in craft jobs, for example as welders.

At the fifth (and largest) integrated steelworks, Scunthorpe, contracting workers such as bricklayers were at work in the blast furnaces and coke ovens, BOS plant and mills. South Yorkshire also had contractors' employees in catering, office cleaning, canteens, building, melting-shop and raw materials stockyard. In the rest of the country (including the Midlands and the North West) contractors were at work in cleaning, security, scrap and slag-handling, and craft refurbishing. It should be noted that, despite the efforts of ISTC and other unions, these lists are not exhaustive and do not give a comprehensive picture of all the work undertaken by contractors throughout BSC.[5]

*Contractors and the redundants.*
Thus far the reader could be forgiven for thinking that I had no colleagues to help me in my efforts to find out about contractors at BSC; this would be quite wrong. While I worked alone as a fieldworker, I was part of a Project with a team of researchers (for a full list of team publications see Harris *et al.*, forthcoming), and even though their research aims were entirely different from my own, my colleagues were also coming across information about contractors. Lydia Morris and Griselda Leaver had been

interviewing samples of those workers made redundant by BSC in 1980 and they had both found, independently, that some of these redundants had had jobs with contractors at the steelworks since their redundancy. Another colleague, Ray M Lee, had administered a much larger survey of a sample of redundant steelworkers and I was able to look at the questionnaires for this survey in order to find out more about redundant steelworkers who went to work for contractors. I had to go back to the original questionnaires because nobody had thought to include information on contracting work in the data that was fed into the University's computer. In fact, it was very difficult to get information on contracting work from the questionnaires themselves: employment details rarely specified whether the firm was a contractor at BSC. But by the time I came to examine the completed questionnaires I already had a list of the main contracting firms at BSC and I used this list, and my knowledge of contracting occupations, to decide which jobs had been with BSC contractors. This was clearly something of a hit-and-miss affair and, when it is added that the job histories on the redundant steelworkers' questionnaires were often incomplete, it is clear the total of redundants with (BSC) contracting experience which I identified was bound to be an under-estimate. It is as well to bear this in mind when looking at the figures below.

When this sample was 'weighted' to replicate the age distribution of *all* the respondents, just under ten per cent of all respondents to the survey of people made redundant from BSC had some experience of contracting work at the steelworks in the two years following their redundancy; however, fifty-five per cent of the total sample had no work at all after their redundancy. The proportion of those redundants finding some work after redundancy who had contracting experience was therefore much higher: over twenty per cent of all the redundants who found work had at least one spell with a BSC contractor.

If the *sample* of redundant steelworkers was representative of *all* those made redundant in 1980, then about 550 of the people made redundant as a result of Slimline worked for a contractor back at the steelworks at some time in the following two years. They were joined in later years by workers made redundant after Slimline. For reasons too complicated to explain here, it may be that the proportion of these later redundants who found work with contractors was even higher than ten per cent (or twenty per cent of those redundants *finding work*). We would therefore estimate that, in total, up to 1,000 of those workers made redundant by BSC between 1979 and 1984 had at least one spell of work with a contractor in the steelworks.

Almost all of the jobs given out to contractors after 1980 consisted of work once done by people BSC made redundant. To put it another way, it was the redundants' jobs that went out to contractors. The redundants themselves explained what had happened in their interviews during the redundancy survey:

'Done away with our janitor's job and gave whole job to contractors.' [Janitor]
  'Department closed and went out to contract labour.' [Mobile Plant Workshop employee]
  'Whole department closed down and was taken over by contractors.' [HGV lorry driver]
  'The whole section finished. Work went out to contractors.' [Painter, Civil Engineering]
  'Whole department except for Chief Surveyor was made redundant. Went to outside firm on contract.' [Senior surveyor]
  'If I remained I thought I would have to take a cut in wages and whole section went shortly afterwards to contractor.' [Mobile Plant operator]
  'Department closed down and it was put out to contract.' [Internal transport driver]
  'My job went. Contractors took it over.' [Burner]
  'The whole job went out to contract.' [Crane driver]
  'The whole Morfa Bank went out to contractors.' [Plant operator, Morfa Bank stockyard]
  'My whole section went. Our work was given to contractors.' [Labour foreman, hot strip mill]
  'The job was coming to a close and being given to contractors.' [Slag tipper, blast furnace]

In some cases the redundant steelworkers 'got their jobs back', although not always the same jobs. Thus one redundant might go back to the steelworks, as a contractors' employee, to do work which was once done by a colleague at BSC. The colleague he replaced might perhaps be doing her/his old job, but as a contracting worker. Thus a man who had been a bricklayer's labourer at BSC might be employed as a rigger in his new life as a contracting worker. In general, however, there was some correspondence between the kind of work redundant steelworkers found with contractors and the kind of work they used to do as BSC employees. Indeed, in some cases, they went back to do exactly the same work.

Explanatory comments on some of the redundant steelworkers' questionnaires showed that in a small number of cases ex-BSC workers found jobs with contractors because their jobs were immediately taken over by contracting firms which made a direct approach with an offer to stay on with their new employer. This was most common amongst drivers of all kinds, mobile-plant operators and janitors. As a manager of a contract cleaning firm explained to me: 'I'm an ex-steelworker myself and, to be honest with you, they're just laying them off and the contractors are taking them on.' Other workers were taken on (*more or less* immediately) to work for contractors in the same job or department — for example, men who had worked in the blast furnaces as electricians or boilermakers, and fitters in heating and ventilating. At Llanwern ex-BSC workers in catering, mobile plant and cleaning performed the same work for contractors. One of the Works Committee members added that 'unfortunately, a lot still think they are working for BSC'!

It seems that BSC still needed the labour of at least some of those workers that had been made redundant. In fact there was an agreement with the steel unions that the contractors should recruit BSC redundants wherever possible. The Slimline document of 15th May 1980 stated

> 'It will be management's concern where Contractors are selected, ... that their immediate manpower needs are identified and where vacancies exist, to use their best endeavours to ensure that Port Talbot Works' employees are recruited.'

According to one of the union negotiators, this clause was the only concession the trade unions managed to extract from management in return for their signatures to the Slimline Agreement. They had originally asked that BSC *guarantee* that contractors would take on redundant BSC workers but the personnel department at Port Talbot would only accept the watered-down version which finally became part of the Agreement. It does not take close inspection to see that this version is full of loopholes and a representative of the contracting employers explained that the clause was merely 'a sop to the unions'. He added, however, that BSC had asked contractors on large new projects, like Concast, to show preference for *local* workers (although not necessarily redundant steelworkers). Even some trade union officials were ambivalent about the recruitment of ex-steelworkers by contractors. Thus at Llanwern the Works Committee had asked contractors to give priority to ex-BSC people but added, 'there's personalities to consider, it's not always a good thing ...'. In fact those redundants who found jobs at BSC Port Talbot with contractors owed their good fortune less to a clause in the Slimline Agreement than to the existence of *make-up pay*.[6]

In 1973, soon after Britain joined the Common Market, BSC had discussions with the EEC about the possibility of financial help to ameliorate the worst effects of the cutbacks in employment then being considered. It is as well, at this point, to establish exactly why

BSC said they wanted EEC money. Even though the areas affected by job losses would include Wales, Scotland and the North of England, BSC did *not* make their case on the basis of the EEC's concern to assist the depressed regions of Europe. Rather, BSC's claim was for assistance to soften the blow resulting from the EEC's efforts to rationalise steel production throughout the member nations. Like agriculture, coal and steel output is controlled at the European level and, since this was an issue arising out of EEC policy on steel output, BSC went to the European Coal and Steel Community (ECSC) to ask for aid. This was *not* a request for assistance of the kind given by the EEC's Social Fund, although readers might be forgiven for thinking it was from the way BSC announced their success in getting hold of ECSC money:

> 'BSC has a sensitive, social conscience ... it has successfully argued the case for enhanced benefits for Welsh and other steelworkers under the terms of the proposed European Coal and Steel Community Re-adaptation Aid Convention'
>
> (Sir Melvyn Rosser, BSC Board member, quoted in *British Steel* Winter 1973/4).

ECSC cash did not arrive in great quantities until seven years later, when BSC began the drastic cutbacks of 1980 at Port Talbot and elsewhere. They told the workers who were going to be made redundant that

> 'Under the European Communities (Iron and Steel Employees Readaptation Benefits Scheme) Regulations 1979 the Government has introduced a scheme for the payment of benefits to certain steelworkers who lose their jobs as a result of particular reductions in activity caused by market conditions in the steel industry.'
>
> 'The British Steel Corporation has agreed to extend similar benefits to other of its employees as defined in agreements between the Corporation and the Trade Unions representing those employees.'

If they could make sense of the literature[7] provided by BSC the prospective redundants would find out there were four ways for them to benefit from ECSC cash. Firstly, they could benefit through early retirement:

> 'If you are a man aged 55 years or more, (50 years for a woman), and you are made redundant, you are entitled to an immediate pension, which can be enhanced by the conversion of Readaptation Benefits.'

Secondly, they might get cash help if they retrained. Approved training gave redundants benefits equal to their previous earnings less tax for a maximum of fifty two weeks.

Thirdly, workers who were unemployed after redundancy benefited. No matter what their real entitlement to State earnings-related supplement (ERS, since abolished of course), they received at least ninety per cent of State ERS on top of unemployment benefit for fifty two weeks of unemployment[8]:

> 'There is a maximum of 52 weeks during which benefits, made up of state ERS and Schemes ERS equivalent, may be paid during unemployment. These weeks, however, need not be continuous providing they fall within the overall period of entitlement of 78 weeks following the date of redundancy.'

Redundants received the same benefits if they were unable to register as unemployed because they were sick. Finally, redundants who found a job or became self-employed had their earnings made up to ninety per cent of their 'previous earnings' at BSC for a maximum of seventy eight weeks: 'Previous earnings' were the average of all normal earnings, excluding non-contractual overtime and payments relating to abnormal working conditions, for the thirteen weeks ending four weeks before redundancy. Current earnings were calculated on a similar basis but over four weeks for employees and six months for the self-employed.

Not all redundants were eligible for these benefits, however. To qualify, a redundant had to be under sixty five (sixty for women) at the date of redundancy and to have been working sixteen hours or more a week for BSC for at least fifty two weeks. Furthermore, s/he had to have worked at the same plant for at least fifty two weeks before the beginning of the change in circumstances which led to her/his redundancy. Finally, s/he must

> 'have been made redundant as defined by the Redundancy Payments Act 1965; now incorporated in the Employment Protection (Consolidation) Act 1978'[9]

and

> 'If you are receiving compensation under the Iron and Steel (Compensation to employees) Regulations 1968 your make up under the Schemes will be adjusted so that your total income does not exceed your previous earnings in the Corporation'.

Even if the redundant worker satisfied the criteria for make-up of pay or benefits, s/he was not paid make-up of earnings if they were absent from their new employment. Furthermore, s/he might lose their entitlement if they left their new job 'through misconduct or without just cause'. The unemployed lost make-up of benefits

> 'for any day on which you are unemployed but are not registered for employment and you are not certified as such; or if you are disqualified or disallowed from receiving State Unemployment Benefit.'

There were some alterations to the 'Schemes' in later years. The maximum period of make-up of unemployment benefit was extended to two years for the over-fifty fives and the level of make-up they received was changed. The under-fifty fives received a maximum of £16 per week for fifty two weeks. The maximum period of make-up of earnings was extended to two years for the over-fifty fives and 130 weeks for the over-sixties. This may be confusing, and it is probably wise to summarise the main point: providing they had not already used up their entitlement while unemployed or on another job or while retraining, ex-BSC workers (under fifty five) who found employment with contractors back at BSC would have their pay made up to a maximum of ninety per cent of their BSC earnings.

In April 1984 the TUC Steel Committee heard that at BSC Ravenscraig, contractors were simply taking over the jobs of men made redundant by BSC and re-employing them at lower wages. They further heard that

'Redundant workers are readily employed by contractors because the men, knowing their wages will be made up ... and cushioned by redundancy pay, are ready to accept low wages'.

ISTC had heard something similar from Scotland a year before:

'Currently the tendency has been to re-employ BSC employees at low rates in the knowledge that the members will receive ECSC make-up.'

But this 'tendency' was not confined to Scotland: a manager of one of the contractors at Port Talbot explained that, since 1980, some contracting firms had paid a 'nominal sum'. The redundant steelworkers accepted low wages because they were glad to have work *and* their pay was made up.

Of course not all of the ex-BSC workers who found employment with contractors had their pay made up. Some had used up their entitlement while unemployed, retraining or in other jobs, and in a *few* cases (see below, Chapters Five and Six) their wages in their new jobs were too high to require make-up to reach ninety per cent of their earnings at BSC. Nevertheless, half of those contracting workers in the survey of BSC redundants said that they received make-up. In fact, data was missing for a third of their number, and we can conclude that more than three-quarters of those who provided information received make-up pay. But what happened when these workers' entitlement to make-up of earnings was exhausted? Their employers certainly did not increase wages to compensate for the loss of make-up. Senior trade union officers explained that BSC would not allow any increase in tenders to allow for a larger wage bill and employers who did attempt to do this lost their contracts. Ex-BSC employees of the contracting firms

complained but most stayed on. As one union official commented,
by this time they were prepared to 'work for a bowl of rice'. This
official had been involved in the contracting story from the start. He
had helped negotiate the clause in the Slimline Agreement which
asked contractors to show preference for redundant steelworkers
and had taken part in subsequent negotiations with BSC over the
use of contractors and in negotiations with the contractors
themselves. His comments provide a useful summary of this
chapter:

> 'The timing of the increase in contracting coincided with the
> redundancies. For example, about 130 lorry drivers went in September
> 1980. Then the contractor came in in October. But the lorry drivers
> were re-employed. The drivers didn't care about the lower wages with
> the contractor because they got their lumper and their make-up. It was
> all very well planned. Obviously the negotiations with the contractors
> began before Slimline was signed.'

In the light of all this evidence, are we correct to refer to the job
losses at BSC as 'redundancies'? Might it not be more accurate to
call them a *mass dismissal*? Other academics have thought about the
meaning of terms like 'redundancy' and 'dismissal'. For example,
Gill Norris (1978) concluded that employers often dismissed people
because of a conflict over how they were employed rather than
because they were not, for instance, 'good workers'. This would fit
in the Port Talbot case, but here more than half the workforce were
'dismissed', hence *mass* dismissal. BSC wanted to employ them in a
different way or, rather, to use their labour without employing them
at all. This recalls a common practice where an individual worker is
dismissed, or threatened with a dismissal, for a breach of discipline.
The employer is prepared to take back the worker if s/he is prepared
to work in the way the employer requires. Thus BSC 'took back'
some of the redundants as the employees of outside contractors.

Surprisingly, the law does not distinguish in any fundamental way
between 'redundancy' and 'dismissal'. In a legal sense, redundancy
is simply one of several (acceptable) *reasons for dismissal*: workers
are dismissed because they are no longer needed rather than, for
example, because of a breach of discipline. Yet the law does allow
workers who have been dismissed to challenge their dismissal in
court by *questioning* the reasons for dismissal. If they are successful,
their dismissal is judged as *unfair* and they are usually awarded
compensation. We have found that many of the workers made
'redundant' by BSC were not redundant at all since the work was
still there even though their jobs (at BSC) were not. Did this
amount to unfair dismissal? After all, the employer changed
working practices and there were new engagements (by the

contractors) under the revised working practices.

Only a specialist labour lawyer would be able to decide whether the Port Talbot redundancies amounted to 'constructive dismissal' (hence unfair dismissal) by BSC, but it is highly unlikely that any tribunal could be persuaded that the mass dismissal at BSC was unfair. If the BSC redundancies were to be judged as unfair dismissals this would set a precedent for many other cases where employers want to change the rules and find redundancy the most convenient way to achieve their aims. The precedent might apply, for example, where companies have moved production from one part of the country to another, or perhaps overseas, in order to take advantage of lower production costs. The workers left behind are supposedly 'redundant' but are really no longer needed only to the extent that the employers wanted to make changes in the way they worked, changes which might in fact constitute breaches of the contract of employment. This is only one example and I'm sure that readers will be able to think of plenty of other cases where the superficial reason for dismissal, 'redundancy', does not hold up on closer inspection. Bob Fryer, an expert in redundancy matters, also refers to redundancies as 'mass' or 'collective dismissal'. Fryer concludes that

> 'it is clear that redundancy short of total closure inevitably entails a reconstruction of labour at the point of production.'
>
> (Fryer, 1981:139).

The following chapter will describe the way in which this 'reconstruction' affected the workers who found jobs with contractors at BSC.

**Footnotes**

1. 'Ex works' contractors are those firms contracted to work for BSC which do not actually perform that work on the BSC site. For example, a contractor may be required to undertake maintenance on some BSC machinery in the firm's own workshop.
2. By this time the steel industry had rather less reason to be envious of the Japanese since Japan's steel production had been falling for some years. In 1986 Japan's steel output fell by nine per cent, the fourteenth consecutive year-to-year decline (*Guardian*, 17 September 1986).
3. Mostly off-site (c.f. Wales TUC, 1976: 138,143).
4. (Appendix three to Slimline Agreement). Note that it is even more difficult to find figures for the numbers of job losses resulting from increases in contracting in individual *occupations*. The appendices to the Slimline Agreement also give the following total job losses: 69 mechanical electrical foremen, 50 technicians, 1140 engineering craftsmen and auxiliaries, 180 electricians, 66 boilermakers and 184 in building occupations (giving a grand total of 1689).
5. A complete list of contractors' work at Scunthorpe, for example, would include canteens, cleaning, thermo-coupling, carpentry, civil engineering, platelaying, mobile plant, opencast mining, labouring groups, sinter plant workers.

6. For further details of the background to, and effects of, make-up see Fevre, 1986a.
7. The quotes in this section are taken from BSC, 1979a.
8. As compared with twenty six weeks of State ERS.
9. BSC had its own schemes for some workers who did not qualify for ESC help because of the *cause* of their redundancy, but still had to be *redundant* as defined here.

Chapter Five

# Working For The Contractors

The preceding chapter showed how, from 1980, BSC brought in increasing numbers of contracting workers in place of direct employees. The contracting workforce was the creation of *two* inter-related demands for labour — from BSC itself and from the firms it contracted to undertake work on its behalf — but the contractors actually paid the wages of the contracting workers. What was it like to work for one of these firms?

*Pay and conditions*
Chapter One suggested that the earnings of contracting workers were lower than the earnings of BSC employees doing comparable work. Local officials of the steel unions were not keen to admit this and liked to claim they could prevent contracting firms paying lower wages through exercising their influence with BSC. At Llanwern it was said that ninety per cent of the skilled contracting workers received the nationally agreed minimum rates for their industry. It was claimed that, in consequence, contracting workers' earnings were 'not so far of' those of BSC employees. The nationally agreed rates for skilled contracting workers were actually higher than those for BSC's skilled employees (£2.60 per hour) although the latter did earn more once bonuses were taken into account and they also had additional fringe benefits like pensions and sickness benefits.

The headquarters of the steel unions were, at least in the early days, influenced by the claims of their local offices. The TUC Steel Committee referred on several occasions to the 'high wages' paid by contractors and concluded that these probably outweighed any loss of fringe benefits. Yet as time went on the detailed replies they received in answer to requests for information from local officers of the constituent unions generally indicated that the earnings of employees of contracting firms were lower than those of BSC employees. This was a fair reflection of the truth[1]: Wyndham Thomas earned £6,100 a year as a BSC employee in 1980 but only £5,800 as a contractor's employee four years later. We have already seen how the earnings of his friend, Barry Kitchen, fell from £7,000 with BSC (Barry was made redundant later than Wyndham) to £6,000 with a contractor. If they had been able to stay at BSC Wyn and Barry would have been earning about £9,000 including premiums and this does not take into account the BSC pension and sick pay. What about the unskilled workers? Peter Smith earned £2 per hour in late 1983. BSC employees doing the same kind of work received a basic £1.99 per hour but shift and other premiums brought their earnings close to £3 per hour. The ISTC's own survey, conducted in 1983, showed how even *basic* wages were dropped when work went out to contract. Cleaners at Newport had earned a basic £1.51 per hour as BSC employees but received £1.47 from the contractor. Catering workers at Ebbw Vale experienced a similar fall to £1.40 per hour. The earnings of amenity attendants had fallen by at least thirty per cent with the transition from BSC to contractors. All of these workers had lost their rights to sick pay and had reduced holiday entitlement.

But surely this was not too bad, not bad for a man or woman made redundant from BSC at any rate? In such cases make-up pay ensured wages were close to what they had been at BSC, the redundancy money was in the bank *and* the 'redundants' had their old jobs back (or, at least, similar ones). Where is the hardship in this? The trade union officials on the Works Committee of one of the BSC plants thought there was little hardship at all. Although their wages were lower with the contractors, the ex-BSC people would not notice because of make-up and their redundancy pay. In fact the redundancy survey conducted by colleagues at Swansea showed that the people who went to work for contractors had not, in the main, worked for BSC for very long. They were too young to have long service records and therefore did not receive the higher redundancy payments. But even if their redundancy money was lower, surely their make-up pay eliminated any suggestion of hardship in the transition from BSC to the contractors? The answer would be 'Yes', except for the fact that a man or woman under fifty-five when made redundant in 1980 would have used up his or her entitlement to make-up pay by the time I interviewed them a couple of years later. They were now subsisting on the contractors' wages alone.

Of course, in a few cases, these wages were high, although it is unlikely that the contracting workers who received higher wages were ex-BSC people because ex-BSC employees rarely found jobs with contracting firms which were party to national agreements on pay and conditions (see Chapter Six). Union officers and officials who negotiated for workers not covered by such agreements faced considerable difficulties, since the 'non-federated' firms paid very low wages and did away with fringe benefits altogether. For example, one union officer wrote to the TUC about the contractors in South Wales, especially at BSC:

'Negotiations with the existing contractors are already a nightmare. A company usually wins the contract by tendering a low price, based on very low wages, and usually no holiday entitlement. It often takes the best part of a year to shame them into giving some holidays and a small increase in wages. By this time the contract is up for renewal, and the contract is won by a new company, again based on low wages and no holidays, and we are off on the merry-go-round once again.'

There is some evidence that, while the earnings of contracting workers were lower than the earnings of BSC employees doing comparable work when work was put out to contract in 1980, the gap between contracting workers' and BSC workers' earnings actually *widened* in subsequent years. The widening gap can be explained by a (relative *and* absolute) *deterioration* in the contractors' pay and conditions. For example, one AUEW official explained that workers used to be able to double their money with the addition of bonus payments. It was now 'almost impossible to do this'. Even though productivity had improved the average bonus had fallen by fifty per cent. On nominated sites, — where the best wages were paid — total earnings had fallen by ten per cent over a decade as a result. Even the employers' representative agreed that earnings had dropped. He thought that contracting employees working on a blast furnace re-line in 1983 would be earning something like seventy per cent of what they might have received nine years before.

The contracting workers' pay and conditions had deteriorated for two reasons. Firstly, they deteriorated because the terms of national agreements covering pay and conditions were no longer so favourable to employees. As the AUEW official's example of falling earnings suggests, changes in the determination of rewards for productivity were central to this process.

Most of the contracting employers were part of the construction engineering industry and the results of their negotiations with the unions were documented in the Mechanical Construction Engineering Agreement dated 1st March 1974. This Agreement lasted, with annual updates, until renegotiation in 1983. It was said that some workers earned a great deal of money — if only for short periods — under the 1974 Agreement. Thus, of the men mentioned in Chapter One, Dick Lewis once received £600 for a six-weeks' spell with one of the contractors on a job near Cardiff. Barry Kitchen says he once made £700 a *week* working for a contractor on a power station in South East England, although to get this much he was working 84 hours a week and the sum included a variety of bonuses including special payments to make sure the contract finished on schedule and allowances for working away from home. Barry also earned good money — although nowhere near as much — working with the same firm on the BSC site at Port Talbot. His mate, Wyndham Thomas, did well in the same job and at one time was getting £120 a week for 'sitting in the house on call'. But of course there were snags — the most important being that the good money never lasted very long. More to the point, circumstances had changed considerably when the Agreement covering these contractors' wages was renegotiated in 1983. Negotiations then took place in the depths of a recession and it was the employers, not the trade unions, who were on the offensive.

The 1983 Agreement (National Joint Council for the Engineering Construction Industry, 1983) retained some of the gains for which the unions had fought in preceding years; however, as one employer said, 'lots of things don't always go by the book' and it was up to the local union organisations to make sure that the Agreement was observed. The Agreement covered the basic week (39 hours), overtime premiums, bonuses for approved welders and heavy crane drivers, holiday pay (for twenty five days plus eight statutory holidays), severance payments, sickness, accident and life assurance benefits, accommodation allowances (including transport expenses) for those working away from home, and 'radius' allowance for those travelling more than two miles to work each day. Some of these clauses only applied to workers who had been employed for a specified period; however, the basic hourly rates of pay applied to all employees covered by the agreement. From 3rd January 1983 these were £3.32 for a skilled working chargehand, £3.15 for a skilled worker, £2.835 for semi-skilled grades and £2.52 for the unskilled. In addition to overtime payments, special bonuses, 'radius' or accommodation allowances, basic pay might also be increased by 'abnormal conditions payments'. These included 'height money', for example, an extra 1.5p per hour if working above fifty feet but under seventy five feet off the ground. The rate could rise to 18p per hour extra for working 250 feet but under 300 feet (although it is clear that the employees who received this bonus could just as easily break their necks with a fall from eighty feet). 'Abnormal conditions payments' also included extra payments for working in confined areas but, in contrast to the 1974 Agreement, there were no longer to be special payments for hot, dirty or muddy conditions. These might be negotiated locally but most firms dropped them as soon as they could. Thus one contractor at BSC Port Talbot no longer paid 18p per hour extra for work around the blast furnace and 12p per hour extra for work around the hot strip mill. They had found these payments were 'abused'; they had become an accepted fact, 'but not any more'.

The biggest difference between the 1974 and 1983 agreements was not concerned with 'abnormal conditions' but with *productivity*. The new agreement brought with it a new deal on shift working and 'second tier' payments for 'productivity', 'co-operation' and 'efficiency'. In fact the new payments represented the employers' attempt to do away with the locally negotiated productivity bonuses which they felt they could now do without. As one of their representatives explained, the contribution of bonus and overtime payments to wages was reduced and workers no longer had their basic wages multiplied several times by these additional payments. In part this reflected an increase in basic hourly rates but there had probably also been a fall in the absolute level of bonus and overtime pay. The new productivity payments were less than the old bonuses and the new shift premiums did not match the old overtime payments. The theory was that workers would do fewer hours, hence less overtime at double or even treble the basic rate, but more shifts. Workers on the first part of a double dayshift (6 am to 2 pm) would receive a twenty per cent premium while workers on the later (2 pm to 10 pm) shift would get a thirty per cent premium. The Concast project at BSC Port Talbot was in fact one of the first in the country to be put on reduced hours (40 and then 39 per week) and double dayshifts, but many employers were able to reduce overtime without introducing shift work.

The Port Talbot survey (see Chapter Six) showed that contracting workers were *less* likely than others to work shifts and few of them earned the shift premiums described in the national agreement. In fact local union officials claim that the changes made for the Concast project at Port Talbot meant more production in fewer 'man hours' but lower earnings. Under the new arrangements 'you may as well stay at home if you were only on day work'. The national drive to improve productivity and reorganise wage structures was distinguished by an uncompromising approach by the employers. As in the other industries where bonus structures were overhauled, the unions complained that the employers would allow no discussion of their proposals. Things were no better at the local level. Thus the industrial relations officer of one contractor at BSC Port Talbot explained that the locally negotiated 37p per hour guaranteed bonus was now years out of date. It should have been renegotiated 'ages ago' but they, in company with other employers, wanted to keep the rate down because they were facing stiff competition in winning contracts. There was little reaction from the unions:

'They grumbled a bit at the time but we've never heard anything since, presumably because of the unemployment.'

The second cause of deteriorating pay and conditions was the increased number of (non-federated) firms not covered by national agreements and therefore not bound to a minimum standard of pay and conditions, however low. Thus, federated firms at BSC Port Talbot paid skilled workers a basic wage of £3.15 per hour plus 37p per hour guaranteed bonus. Some workers — especially those on the 'nominated' projects where auditors were appointed — also received the extra payments detailed in the NJCECI Agreement, for example, severance pay of £2.50 for each week worked and holiday credits of £16 per week. Skilled workers in the non-federated firms received none of the fringe benefits and relied on a (basic) wage of between £2 and £2.50 per hour. Firms outside engineering construction paid similar rates, for example, £2.20 per hour for a diesel fitter working on a contractor's fleet of lorries used for internal transport at BSC.

In 1984 the federated firms raised their basic hourly rates for skilled workers to £3.30 per hour but the locally negotiated bonus remained the same, except for contractors on BSC's hot strip mill project who agreed to pay a bonus at nearly double the old rate. Other fringe benefits in the federated firms were as before. Again non-federated firms were able to do without fringe benefits and could pay lower basic rates. Thus Barry Kitchen and Wyndham Thomas were paid £2.79 per hour with a 'special rate' of £4 per hour for overtime. This 'special rate' works out at less than 'time and a half' yet they explained that their employer insisted they should work bank holidays at £4 per hour if they wanted to get overtime in future. Barry also complained that he did 'two men's jobs — fitting *and* welding' — for his £2.79. If he complained, the boss simply said that there were plenty of blokes on the dole who wanted the job.

Wages for semi-skilled and unskilled workers were of course even lower, although in federated firms these workers received at least £2.50 per hour. Others received half this rate and, again, there were no fringe benefits. One ISTC officer thought that BSC had 'double standards' in relation to wage rates. BSC made money available so that the contractors could pay the agreed rates for the engineering construction industry but not for the non-craft workers, the semi-skilled and unskilled. Similarly with conditions and fringe benefits. Thus contract cleaners gave their employees only twenty days' holiday as against twenty eight when employed by BSC.

When reading these details of pay and conditions, readers should note that they do not fully describe the plight of the contracting workers. Perhaps the most important point to remember is that the contracting workers' wages (whether paid by a federated or a non-federated firm) were *irregular*. We have seen something of the contracting workers' conditions of employment — the absence of pensions, sick pay and paid holidays, for example — but arguably the most important aspect of these conditions was the *insecurity* of contracting employment (and the absence of monetary compensation for that insecurity).

According to one AUEW official, in the good old days of the 1950s you were never out of work for longer than a month. If you hadn't had work for six weeks you would think it 'ridiculous'. When in work, the contract might last for anything from three months to three *years*. Of course the memory fades, but there is no doubt that even in more recent times many contracting workers could count on working for the greater part of the year, *especially* if they were prepared to move around. There were still 'travelling men' in the industry since the industry still required them:

> 'It is a condition of your employment with the Company that you must, if so instructed, transfer from site to site anywhere in the United Kingdom in continuance of your contract of employment'.
>> (Extract from the Contract of Employment
>> used by a Port Talbot contracting firm).

In theory, travelling men in continuous employment (on *nominated* projects) with federated firms could still earn good money. Workers who complied with the extract clause above could add twenty per cent to their annual earnings by moving around with this firm. But, as the production manager pointed out, they could no longer expect continuous employment. They were now more likely to work for eight months a year rather than ten:

> 'If they are unemployed now it's not from their own choosing. It's different now, none of the big projects ...'

Travelling men might, if they were lucky, work for two-thirds of the year but they were the 'elite', the favoured minority. The rest were simply paid off at the end of the contract for which they were engaged.

We have already noted that the NJCECI agreement allowed for the payment of severance pay of £2.50 for each week worked to employees, for a specified period, in order to compensate for the lack of job security which was endemic to the industry. As one employer put it:

> 'It is a special arrangement to make up for getting laid off so often.'

The Secretary of the Federation explained that redundancy never caused any 'hue and cry' because people expected it. They knew they were going to get a month's work, two years if they were one of a small, and very lucky minority (with a week's pay in lieu for their two years' service). In fact the NJCECI agreement had something further to say about job 'security'. Firstly, continuous employment for four weeks guaranteed the worker a thirty nine hour week

(except for agreed short time), that is if s/he had *not* worked for four
weeks, Monday morning might bring the news that there was no
work that week and they should come back on Friday! Four weeks'
continuous employment also guaranteed a week's notice (only two
*hours'* notice was required up to this time) and the severance pay of
£2.50. In the highly unlikely event that a worker had been employed
for more than two years they received no severance pay since they
were then entitled to (statutory) redundancy pay. Of course even
the statutory protection of redundancy legislation did not always
work for these few 'long-serving' employees. For example, a South
Wales contractor was found guilty of not correctly consulting the
relevant trade unions over redundancies. (As seems quite common,
these redundancies took place just before Christmas.) The plant
manager spoke at the hearing:

> 'He said they had very little notice of this decision and the result was
> that the Company had no option but to make the men redundant.
>    'With very little prior warning of the termination of contracts,
> Mr ----- said the company could not consult on the subject of
> redundancies as effectively as it would wish to.'
>                              (*South Wales Evening Post*, 14 March 1984)

Most contracting workers worked for much shorter spells than
the two years which were required for protection under the
redundancy legislation. Thus one of the Port Talbot contracting
firms I visited had just hired seventy men for three *days'* work. The
last time they paid off a large number of workers, 450 men were
involved and none qualified for redundancy pay. This was not, in
fact, a contract at the steelworks; however, contracts as short as this
were given out by BSC. ISTC local officials throughout Britain
reported that most contracts lasted a year, rarely longer. Other
contracts lasted for a couple of weeks, or even days, or 'as
required'. At Llanwern, for example, it was said that the craftsmen
'come and go' all the time. The same could be said of labourers
working on repair and maintenance — for example, on shutdowns
and stop weeks — and other work. The maximum length of contract
was one year for cleaners and the like; many other contracts only
lasted for two or three months and an ISTC officer in South Wales
reported that BSC were increasing their use of these very short
contracts in preference to year-long arrangements.

Realistically, the best a manual worker looking for work with a
contractor at BSC could expect to get was a year-long contract with
the *hope* that the firm would win the contract again at the end of the
year. This is, as one ISTC official reported to his head office in 1983,
completely unpredictable:

> 'We have the task of representing members who were, in the main,

ex-BSC employees and now find themselves in a "different world", i.e. low earnings, (not all cases) poor Conditions of Employment, with the continual threat that they may not be employed next year, i.e. Loss of Contract.'

Of course, a year-long contract which *may* be renewable is better than a one-off job which, when completed, will not be put out to tender again. Nevertheless, it is as well to bear in mind that the contract between BSC and the contractor did not give the contractors' *employees* secure employment for a year. They could *hope* they were kept on for the full term but they did not know this; in other words, they did not even have the degree of security of a temporary worker with a fixed-term contract of employment with his employer. Thus heavy cleaners like Dick Lewis had 'no security whatsoever' since an order was put in for their labour for five days at a time.

In the main, *skilled* contracting workers were less likely to be employed on jobs where their employer had a year-long contract or one which was renewable. The nature of their labour meant that it was more likely they would be working on one-off jobs like repairs. Yet these skilled workers were more likely to get the opportunity to stay with a firm at the end of contract, although, even if work outside BSC is considered, such opportunities were rare. The unfortunate thing was that they, like the semi-skilled or unskilled workers, never knew how long their job was going to last. As the employers' representative explained, 'temporary people' are not taken on as temporary employees: 'no distinction is made at the time of engagement'. The employers themselves confirmed this: although they might try to give a 'rough idea' the job could last for anything from a few weeks to a couple of months — 'it depends what happens'. Frank Clark rarely knew how long his employer's contract was scheduled to last (or whether other contracts were in the offing), let alone how long he could expect *his* job to last. The foreman might tell him what to expect but he usually had to rely on his own powers of observation — 'you can usually tell when the work starts drying up' — for early warning of the end of a job. Even though he had been with one firm for over six months, Frank was never able to establish the kind of relationship with his foreman which would have given him more reliable information on when the job would end. The insecurity of contracting work remains even for those employees with the longest service records. Thus one manager explained that his firm had a few men who had been with them for eight years who were still 'temporary' and could be paid off next week.

Throughout his (short) time with a contractor at BSC, Peter

Smith was aware that he could be told at any time to go home or not to bother coming in tomorrow. Although this might mean he was permanently out of the job (as eventually happened), this could also be a temporary layoff, that is his employer did not guarantee to employ him for a whole week. He compared his position to that of the BSC men he worked next to: they had 'guaranteed hours' even though they might refuse to work extra shifts; and when he was not working too *few* hours, Peter was working too *many*. Some local union officials say the same about hours as about wages: they insist that *BSC* insist that the contracting workers' hours are in line with those of BSC employees — over-long hours for contracting workers have been stamped out. But at Port Talbot, at least one official was prepared to admit that contracting workers were still doing up to sixteen hours a day: 'they get people in one day a fortnight who have to stay till they finish'. My survey of ISTC officials uncovered other examples of contracting workers doing well over the agreed maximum of forty hours. This was certainly the case with Peter Smith.

When Peter began work for a contracting firm at BSC he worked a straight twelve-hour day from 6 am to 6 pm. The firm later changed the job to a three-shift (eight hours each) system; however, his usual week was seventy six hours and he had worked 101 on one occasion. In fact, when the three-shift system began he had to do two shifts in a row on the first day. First he was told not to come in when he had expected to start work at 6 am, then he got a 'phone call telling him to see the foreman at 2 pm. He turned up in his best clothes (although he had taken his working clothes just in case) and was told he had to work from then until 6 am the next morning. They had decided to start the three-shift system — although he had not been forewarned — but did not have the necessary cover for the first shift and couldn't be bothered calling in an extra man to do it. It was this practice which made long hours an accepted norm even on the three-shift system: Peter would be told at any time to come in and do 'overtime'. The job had to be covered for twenty four hours so if someone were sick, for example, Peter had to go in. It seems that many of the jobs we are describing here — jobs in which you can turn up in the morning not knowing if you will work a full day or a double shift — might accurately be called *casual work*. Here's Peter Smith again:

> 'Most contractors like to take you on as casual first of all. The proportion as casual would be about half and half. The casual workers get lower pay and there are less overheads.'

We will shortly return to the question of casual work, after a brief summary of the findings of this section. Firstly, contracting workers' pay and conditions were worse than for comparable work as BSC employees. Secondly, contractors' pay and conditions had deteriorated for two reasons. In the first place employers had gained the upper hand in agreements which set official standards for pay and conditions. In the second, fewer employers were party to such agreements and they were able to offer even worse pay and conditions to their employees. Finally, we saw that all contracting work was insecure.

This summary could also stand as a summary of the feelings expressed by the contracting workers themselves. Workers with experience of contracting work who were included in the Port Talbot survey (see Chapter Six) were generally dissatisfied with pay. They were also more likely to say that their current or last job (with a contractor) was worse than most jobs they had had. (Contracting workers interviewed in the *redundancy* survey were also unenthusiastic about their jobs). Finally, contracting workers in the Port Talbot survey were more likely than others to say their current job (if in work) was insecure, and were even more dissatisfied with conditions of employment, including job (in)security than they were with pay.

*Work 'off-the-books'*
It is usually assumed that casual work — such as that described by Peter Smith — is done 'off the books': the employer does not admit to employing the casual worker and the 'employee' pays no tax or national insurance contributions. In contracting work the assumption that casual work is 'off the books' was frequently correct. In the Port Talbot survey men with experience of contracting work were far more likely than the other men in the sample to admit that they had worked off the books. As Peter Smith explained:

> 'You can get casual work straight in hand. You can do it if they want cover — a day or so but not indefinitely.

As we will see below, some of this off-the-books work actually lasted much longer than the odd day or so, and it would be foolish to think that it is rare. It is possible, in fact, that twenty five or thirty per cent of work for BSC contractors since 1980 has been off the books.

In 1983/4 the going rate for this work was between £10 and £15 a day. Even if unemployment benefit was claimed at the same time, these rates would make it very difficult for a worker to average a total income of £100 a week. It should not be assumed, however, that all of the workers concerned claimed State benefits — either unemployment, supplementary or sickness — and some sources suggested a majority did not. Those who didn't claim while working were earning only a bit more than they would have received in benefits. The best hourly rate they could expect was between £1.80 and £1.90 and it is clear that the absence of the normal deductions from pay was more than balanced by a rate of less than sixty per cent of the wages of workers employed in the normal way.

Barry Kitchen explained that 'cash in hand' from the contractors actually came in a normal pay envelope but not marked in the usual way with the employee's name on the front. Barry had worked beside men who were paid in this way, at £1.50 an hour, doing heavy cleaning on the downshift at BSC. Most off-the-books work tended to be hard, and it might also involve long hours. But, as one union official pointed out, this was a way of bringing earnings up to a reasonable level: with twelve-hour night shifts a worker *might* take home £100 a week off-the-books. This official added that off-the-books work was now so widespread that the practice had even affected occupations like surveying where hourly rates were higher and long hours unnecessary.

The *employers* gained from 'employing' people off-the-books because it was cheaper to do it that way. Thus the contractor might charge BSC for the labour of forty men at the full hourly rate whereas half of them would be off-the-books earning £10 a day[2]. This is, as will be explained below, much less of a risk for the firm than the workers involved. For a worker off-the-books there is always a risk:

> 'There's a man from Cwmavon and he knew the Social suspected something. The only day he didn't work was the Wednesday he signed on ... The rest of the time he was watched. What he had to do was, every morning he got his push bike, cycle up to the Bwlch, down the other side into Baglan, go down the cycle lane; go down the motorway so if they came after him *he* could turn round but they'd have to go right down before they could turn round and by the time they'd done that he'd be gone back to Baglan where his lift would pick him up in a back street ... He did that for £10 a day ... never did get caught. I'd be too afraid'.

A man might not risk a fine or imprisonment and cycle up and down a mountain and a motorway for £10 a day on top of his State benefit, but he might take the risk to avoid having no income at all. This is easy to explain once the supplementary benefit rules are clear: a man or woman signing off the unemployment register for a short spell of employment would disqualify themselves from receipt of benefit for a spell after they became unemployed once more. In fact, the short spell of work might actually mean no net gain in income at all — they would have been in just the same financial position had they remained on supplementary benefit (also see

Ferman et al., 1984). As Peter Smith pointed out, the ideal was a job which lasted for thirteen weeks. In this case you qualified for unemployment benefit and the delay between becoming unemployed and receiving your first benefit payment was much shorter:

> 'You *have* to make sure the job lasts for at least thirteen weeks to make it worth while ... But you *can't* make sure, it's pot luck. When I started I thought it would be casual, but they said it had to be on the books'.

*This* was the natural alternative, of course: if the job was not going to last for thirteen weeks you could only be sure of your benefit entitlement at the end of the job if you continued to claim while working. Off-the-cards work is — with the help of the rules for benefit claims — a direct product of the *insecurity* of work with contractors. This is also clearly the case where workers are offered work for one day only. If this work is on the books the workers may well lose their benefit for the whole week and employers were sometimes surprised to find the offer of a shift's work refused for this reason.

*Self-employed* workers had other reasons to seek off-the-books work. On the first day of work the contractor's foreman or engineer might tell the workers — usually skilled — with self-employed forms that there was no need to declare the work, that is, it was not going to appear in the firm's books. They would therefore continue to claim benefit but also avoid all the paperwork involved in self-employment[3]. Calculations based on cash alone are not the only factor affecting the decision to accept work off the books. It's not just guilt or fear but *shame* that prevents some workers from doing so, and which the rest have to put up with. Furthermore, off-the-books work is low status to say the least. All in all, if you haven't found out that you will lose money by doing so, you will try to turn an off-the-books job into a real one because it makes you feel better. You feel even better when you can sign off the dole and, of course, should you have a chance of a 'permanent' job you can now tell your prospective employer you have been in work.

As we might expect, the officials of the steel trade unions were the most optimistic about the chances of stamping out off-the-books work. They began by saying it wasn't that common and was nothing new but added that BSC 'frown on this' and would kick out any contractor caught with 'lump labour'. (As one ex-BSC manager explained, 'kick out' really means that the contractor is not invited to tender again.) They were not 'one hundred per cent sure' that they had been able to stamp out off-the-books work but they had only had eight or nine cases reported. This is, of course, the problem: in order for BSC to 'kick out' the offending contractor, somebody has to tell them what is going on. There is, in fact, no reason why BSC should go to any trouble to find out if off-the-books labour is being used; as Derek Rees, the ex-manager, pointed out, on a lump-sum contract BSC simply want the work done quickly and don't care how it's done. This was confirmed by an ISTC officer who reported the following conversation with a senior BSC executive at Port Talbot. The executive had told him that BSC knew what was going on and didn't care as long as they got the cheapest labour going:

> 'He said to me, "Malcolm, we used to have a social conscience. We don't have a social conscience any more. It's like this, we take the cheapest labour we can ...".'

As is usual with the steel trade unions, the lay officials and the full-time officers differed in the degree of frankness with which they answered questions. Unlike the officials, the full-time officer could admit that off-the-books work was going on without creating doubts about his own authority. The lay officials preferred to pretend they had influence with BSC and were in a position to prevent such things as off-the-books work. In practice the workers felt that only one or two of the unions were taking positive steps to combat off-the-books work. One of these was the AUEW but, as an official of that union explained, they could do little without the co-operation of the workers involved. They would not admit that they had been working off the books until they were caught, and even then they might not name the firm for fear of being blacklisted in future. They also suspected that, no matter what they said, the firm would get off lightly. The AUEW official thought there was some truth in this. Even if both parties were fined, this meant little to the employer but a great deal to the worker who would also have to pay back the benefits he or she had claimed. In fact, the employer might not be punished at all. Thus the official had dealt with one case where the offending firm had actually 'shopped' a man working off the cards. The man sought the assistance of the union and explained that he had worked with the contractor on a job at BSC Port Talbot (on a blast furnace) for eight weeks in 1981. He had only been on the books for two of these weeks. When the Department of Health and Social Security (DHSS) investigated him the firm claimed he had been on the books all the time: now who would be stupid enough to claim benefit while they were actually working on the books? The DHSS didn't think of this, apparently, and the man got a £500 fine; the firm 'got off scot-free'.

Barry Kitchen has some experience of working off-the-books. He did it for £15 a day for one of the heavy cleaning contractors at BSC Port Talbot, and was able to ascertain that the head office of the firm 'knew about it'. He had some trouble on the job and threatened to 'tell the dole' about them. The local people gave him the name and telephone number of the big boss and Barry rang up — they knew all about him. In fact the big boss was never in when Barry rang and so he never got the chance to complain, and he didn't tell the dole either when he went down to sign on the following day. ('I'm not that kind of bloke'). Barry thought the authorities 'do a deal with the firms: they let the firm off as long as they catch the men'. This meant that the firm could begin again after a while:

> 'A couple of months keeping quiet, doing the odd job with their regular gang, then they fetch another lot in, not the same lot who got caught of course'.

Barry had little faith in the effect of DHSS clampdowns: they simply put a temporary break on the practice. It might be easy to catch men on a big shutdown at BSC at Christmas or August when six or eight hundred men 'live there for a fortnight', but it was much easier for the contractors to get away with it when working a fortnightly downshift. The union officials who *are* concerned about off-the-books work agreed: DHSS clampdowns simply proved how much of this went on rather than helped to eliminate it. It may be that the DHSS also agreed:

> 'The lump — it's just a tip of the iceberg':
> 'A group of local labourers and tradesmen working at the Port Talbot steelworks' Concast plant for a sub-contractor were taking advantage of a supplementary benefits' fraud known colloquially as the "lump", Afan magistrates heard ...
> 'Mr Richard Evans, prosecuting for the DHSS ... said all the defendants joined the trade union UCATT to enable them to work for sub-contractor Patrick McGinley at BSC Port Talbot, and each of the men worked under a false name.
> 'He said the use of the false names made the fraud almost impossible to detect, but Mr Evans praised the vigilance and detective work of local DHSS investigators in bringing the men and their crimes to light ...
> 'Said Mr Evans: "These men were operating a DHSS fraud known colloquially as the 'lump' and I would submit that what you see before you today is but a tip of the iceberg".
> 'Mr Alan Roper, defending ... said his client was a victim of the poverty trap, whereby hire-purchase, mortgage and other household bills were mounting up at a time when he was desperately looking for work to keep his wife and two children.
> 'Said Mr Roper: "My client, through no fault of his own, was out of work for 15 months before falling to the temptation which brought him to court today."

'----- was fined a total of £120 on three charges of false representation and two offences were taken into consideration. He was also ordered to pay £399.22 compensation ...

'----- ----- who worked using the name "Geoff Davies", was fined a total of £80 on two false representation charges. Mr Evans said he received £42.30 to which he was not entitled and later repaid it.

'----- told the court: "I had been unemployed for some time so when this chance came along I had no hesitation about taking it".'

*Port Talbot Guardian*, 12 May 1983)

### Finding work with the contractors

Finding a job with the contractors — even a legitimate job on-the-books — was not something one could go about in the 'normal' way through letters of application and the good offices of the Job Centre. Most contractors' vacancies could not be filled through the Job Centre or through newspaper advertisements because these methods were too slow. Their demand for labour (like their frequent need to dispense with labour) was immediate. Yet contracting workers had to find work more frequently than any other group, precisely because their jobs lasted for such a short time and they were so frequently out of work. So great was the effort put into job search, and so frequently did they have to make this effort, that finding work with the contractors should rightly be considered as part of the conditions of contracting work.

Finding a job with a contractor, as with any employer, involved two tasks — learning about a vacancy and landing the job. As far as most contracting work is concerned, both tasks were accomplished using *informal* means. A 'social network' of friends, acquaintances and relatives[4] could be of some help in providing information about vacancies. Such a network could save time and legwork since the only alternative was to contact all the prospective employers in turn. It was also a more effective — as well as a more efficient — way of finding out about vacancies since the employers' demand for labour was so immediate. By simply contacting each employer in turn a worker could have very little chance of making contact at the precise moment a vacancy had arisen. But good information was not sufficient to guarantee success in the search for work with the contractors.

Some contractors moved in to BSC while the people who were to be made redundant were still at work. These firms were able to recruit their labour force amongst the redundants:

'Contractor took over department and I was promised a job.'

'Promised a job, name put forward.'

'Contractor gave forms to us.'

'The contractors were working there before I finished and I applied for the job.'

'Job was offered me. Firm of contractors approached me. I'm doing the same job.'

Other contracting firms faced more difficult recruitment problems. Their difficulties did not arise from a *shortage* of candidates for vacancies, but from an *excess* of prospective employees — how were they to select the best candidates? Normal procedures could be ruled out because the jobs were too short-term to make such procedures worthwhile, or because members were needed so quickly as to make such procedures useless. Yet, like the computer company ('Griffin') in Chapter Three, the contractors were faced with a bewildering task: how were they to select workers from such an army of prospective employees? The answer lay in *informal* selection procedures.

Informal selection procedures lifted a burden from the employers and placed it firmly on the shoulders of their prospective employees. Instead of the employer diverting time and resources to interviewing and selection, the worker was required to put in time and effort to distinguish him/herself from the crowd. Chapter One included some examples of the use of social networks to achieve this end. Social networks could be used to actually land the job — for example where a friend could *bestow* employment — or, more frequently, to provide a (verbal) reference which might lift the candidate out of the crowd but would not guarantee employment[5]. Instances of both uses of social networks appeared in the *redundancy* survey when ex-BSC workers were asked why they had been hopeful of alternative employment when they were made redundant:

'Because I had friends in contractors' firms.'
  'My friend has a contracting firm.'
  'A friend was an agent and he helped me to get the job.'
  'My mate started his own firm. He was looking for men and he asked me to work for him.'
  'My father got me in.'

Without an effective social network, or, frequently, *in addition* to one, contracting workers used personal visits to prospective employers to make themselves known *and* to present themselves as suitable employees. Thus, when out of work, Frank Clark visited all the firms he had worked for even though he was already 'on their books'. (He found personal visits more effective than telephone calls). Even when — as in Frank's case — the worker had experience with several different contractors, and all of these firms kept 'call lists' of former and prospective employees, a contracting worker would still want to do everything in his/her power to distinguish him/herself from the crowd. Personal visits or social networks were used to let prospective employers know not only that he or she was available, but also to inform employers of the worker's characteristics (his/her ability, attitude and trustworthiness). If we look at Frank Clark's methods of finding work in a little more detail, the reader should get some idea of the lengths to which contracting workers were prepared to go — and *had* to go — to find employment[6]. The following narrative should illustrate all of the major points made so far: the use of informal sources of information about vacancies, the use of informal methods to land a job, and the sheer *effort* put into job search by contracting workers.

In the autumn of 1984, I went looking for a job with Frank Clark. Frank had just been paid off by one contractor at BSC and wanted to visit some of the other firms on the steelworks site to see if they had any work for him. In particular, he had been given a 'tip-off' about a possible job with a firm which I will call SJP. We drove into the BSC by the least frequented entrance, thus reducing the risk of a check by the security men who are meant to prevent anyone without business with BSC or the contractors getting into the steelworks, and arrived at the SJP 'cabin' twenty minutes early. Frank took the opportunity to call in at another contractor's to 'get forms' in order to make an application for work there. The SJP cabin was still empty when he returned so Frank left a note for the boss, 'Mr Mathias', asking him to ring Frank at home if he wanted him. I suggested we should call back later but Frank said the bloke had had his chance and could ring if he wanted.

Later on we went to look for a (low-level) BSC manager who, Frank told me, had 'been good' to him, and I found out there was more to the apparently off-hand way in which Frank left the note at the SJP cabin than had appeared at the time. It turned out that it was the BSC man who had given him the 'tip' about the job and, in fact, had 'put in a good word' for him. But the BSC man had told Frank that Mr Mathias would probably only be able to offer him *one day's* work. Frank hadn't told me anything about this before. He now said he realised he didn't really want one day's work, it wasn't 'much use' to him, but he had been worried that if he hadn't gone to see Mr Mathias he would have lost the goodwill of his friend the BSC manager. In fact his friend was able to put Frank's mind at rest. Frank told me that he said

> "Don't worry, it's no reflection on you. I tell you frankly, *I* wouldn't do it. If he only offers you one day and you don't want it, tell him."

In other words, Frank could now turn down the job without ruining his chances of help from the BSC man in future, but what would this do for his chances of another job with SJP, and for the credibility of his BSC friend as a 'referee' in the eyes of Mr Mathias? Frank was now in two minds as to whether to go back to SJP's cabin. He wanted to believe the BSC manager but wasn't at all sure that he wouldn't lose his chances of work with SJP altogether by turning down one day's work. He now explained that the day in question was *tomorrow*. Frank already had something planned and if he left it up to Mr Mathias to contact *him* he wouldn't call in time. Frank would therefore be spared the difficulty of changing his plans and, more to the point, would not be put in a position where he would either have to work the one day or risk ruining his future chances by turning the job down. In the end, Frank decided to go back to the SJP cabin and there was Mr Mathias getting out of his Rover. Frank went to speak to him and came back smiling: 'It was OK. I *knew* him.'

Because Frank already knew Mr Mathias — and, more to the point, Mr Mathias already knew Frank — Frank could afford to turn down the one-day job offer without losing the chance of another job with SJP. In fact, Mathias had told Frank he had *two* shifts' work coming up soon. Although this might not seem much better than one day — and would still only earn Frank £50 gross — Frank said it was a better offer. At least this would make it worthwhile, and maybe he could have a word with the other boys on the job and see whether they bothered signing off the dole to do it. In fact, he would have taken even the one day if it had been altogether 'off the cards' but Mr Mathias had said 'No'. Frank could see why: SJP 'pays from away'. They couldn't have people off the books because head office would think the local manager was pocketing the extra money (over and above the wages for his legitimate workforce) provided for wages.

Before any reader begins to censure Frank Clark's morals, let he or she remember that Frank's indecision about the one-shift job with SJP followed from his reluctance to be seen to turn down *any* sort of work. In Frank's working world what is important is that you should be seen to be willing to work, whatever the job and whatever its status — on or off the cards. Of course Frank was also trying, in the face of some difficult circumstances, to retain a sense of his own *worth*. He is a craftsman, and has *never* left a job voluntarily: could he sell his labour casually by the day or the shift and for only £50? Frank didn't know where to draw the line. Somehow the situation might be salvaged if he could get the £50 and unemployment benefit as well; then the work would be simply something extra, not his whole reward, his whole worth[7].

Stories like Frank Clark's suggest that some workers in modern Britain find themselves in circumstances which recall the situation at the beginning of this century. In 1909 W M Beveridge described the casual worker as being

> 'the rock upon which all hopes of thrift and self-help or trade union organisation, no less than all schemes of public assistance, are shattered.'

Together with casual work, Beveridge also hoped to put an end to

> 'the aimless, unguided search for work which is involved in the hawking of labour from door to door.'
>
> (Quoted by Fryer, 1981: 145-6).

But the contractors had little use for the successors of Beveridge's 'labour exchanges' — the Job Centres — and the workers paid the price for this neglect when they undertook their desperate and often hopeless search for work.

**Footnotes**

1. We are now used to the observation that inequalities in earnings have increased because of changes in the tax burden of different income groups (compare to *Guardian* 8 February 1984), but this information should remind us that the gap between the well-paid and the low-paid may also increase because of changes in relative wages.
2. I am indebted to Griselda Leaver for this information and for allowing me to reproduce the extract from her interview notes which follows.
3. The more sophisticated strategies used to hide off-the-books work usually involve spurious 'self-employment' which keeps the contracting firm in the clear. Thus an imaginary firm will be used as a sub-contractors while the work is actually done by a group of men working off the books. As one union officer put it: 'there are joking firms in the Abbey', (i.e. BSC, Port Talbot).
4. And, in some cases, the help of a local trade union organisation.
5. Using social networks was not cost-free. Formal recruitment methods cost employees time and money and informal job search can cost workers more than this: they are, in a sense, *in hock* to their friends and relatives.
6. Even Frank Clark could be outdone in the pains he took to land a contracting job: some contracting workers worked without wages for a week so that their prospective employers could assess their suitability.
7. If the reader should wonder how I can claim to read Frank's mind so well, he or she can guess that Frank is very good at explaining his feelings or that I have experienced exactly the same dilemma he was going through that day at the steelworks.

Chapter Six

# An Irregular Army

We now know a little about contracting work, but we know next to nothing about the workers who perform it. The fitters' stories in Chapter One provided very unsystematic 'evidence' and later chapters have simply shown that a proportion of contracting workers had been made redundant by BSC. It is therefore fortunate that, from the outset, it was intended that the project on which I worked at University College of Swansea would include a survey of men living in Port Talbot. By the time this survey was being designed, it was already clear that questions about people's experience of work with contracting firms would be useful. The questionnaires therefore included questions on whether the interviewee (or 'respondent') had worked for a BSC contractor at any time in the last ten years, whether they did so in their last or current job, and whether they did so in their main occupation between 1969 and 1978.

The survey revealed three trends which had affected many men in the sample and, therefore, had also affected many men in the town as a whole. Firstly, some workers had suffered 'downward social mobility', that is they had moved from higher ranked occupations to lower ones. Secondly, some men in the sample had been affected by falling incomes. Thirdly, the sample had been affected by rising unemployment. While all three of these trends had affected men who had had no experience of work with contracting firms, their effects were *most* marked for the men with such experience. That is, the contracting workers were like the sample as a whole, only *more* so. In order to demonstrate this we need to know a little about the sample as a whole, and then a little about the different *sub*-groups of contracting workers.

Just over half of the 294 men interviewed were skilled manual workers. A fifth were currently employed by BSC Port Talbot and an additional sixteen per cent had worked for BSC in their last job. Just over three-quarters of all those working were trade union members and a majority of working non-members had been so in the past. Nearly two-thirds of the sample were owner-occupiers but sixty per cent of the men were Labour supporters (the constituency within which Port Talbot lies produced a Labour majority in excess of 15,000 at the 1983 general election).

These few details make Port Talbot sound like a skilled, affluent, 'solid working-class' town, but this is an illusion. Of those who provided information — in fact, a quarter did not — nearly half of the men reported that the net income of their household was less than £112.69 per week. In fact more than one in ten said that weekly net income was less than £56.40.

The survey was undertaken in 1984, four years after the major BSC redundancies and the doubling of male unemployment. The solid working-class town was by then a thing of the past. In the present, or at least over the years 1978 to 1984, *forty per cent* of the sample had experienced redundancy. *Only sixty per cent* were in some form of employment. A little under a fifth were unemployed and available for work and half of these — one in ten of the whole sample — had been out of work for more than two years. The remainder of the sample were older workers who had 'withdrawn' from the labour market and were not included in the employed or unemployed groups. Some of these men had been forced to give up all idea of finding work by, for example, ill health. Others had soberly assessed their chances of further employment and decided they would remain without work for the rest of their lives. They therefore found some other status (than unemployment), for example 'early retirement'.

The households of the unemployed were less likely than the households of the employed group to contain *any* employed adult and so their household incomes were very low. One in three of the unemployed who answered reported a net household income of under £56.40 per week and the vast majority (eighty- four per cent) reported household incomes below £112.69. Two-thirds of the unemployed men lived in council houses — as against a quarter of those in work — and only six per cent of their households had a relatively new car.

The currently unemployed also differed from the employed in less obvious respects (than income and wealth). They were *younger* for one thing. Just over half (fifty-five per cent) of the unemployed were under thirty four as against thirty-nine per cent of those currently in work. The unemployed had less training and qualifications. Seven out of ten had no formal qualifications, as against about half of those currently in work, and only a quarter (thirty-seven per cent for the employed group) had attempted apprenticeships. Nevertheless, some of the unemployed *were* skilled, yet their skills appeared to provide no defence against unemployment.

The unemployed *were* lower than the employed in terms of occupation and 'social class' (according to their last job). Hardly any of the unemployed fell into 'social classes' I, II or III (non-manual) used by the Registrar General whereas 47 per cent were classified as 'social class' III (skilled manual), 28 per cent as 'social class' IV (semi-skilled manual) and 22 per cent as 'social class' V (unskilled manual)[1]. It seems that, as we would expect, the men who were unemployed at the time of the survey were over-represented in those categories where labour supply was most likely to exceed the demand for labour, but more detailed analysis shows that some of the men in the unemployed group *used to be* higher up the occupational ranking. These men slipped down the ranking because their skills, typically related to *manufacturing* work, were apparently no longer in demand. Unlike other similar groups, these men found they were unable to use their skills or qualifications to re-establish themselves and they slipped down into the more vulnerable semi-skilled or unskilled occupations (including 'contracting occupations' — see below) where unemployment was more likely. Other workers, with different skills, were able to move up, or at least across, the occupational order. They suffered less from the general drop in demand for the labour of skilled manual workers because, although they no longer put into practice the training they had received (in apprenticeships for example) they were nevertheless able to move into jobs where the competition for employment was less intense.

Some men in the unemployed group had slipped down the occupational hierarchy and so had become vulnerable to unemployment, but we should not conclude that the rest of the unemployed — those men without training or qualifications — were in any sense 'unemployables'. Of the whole unemployed group, eighty-four per cent had been in work and most of the remainder were recent school-leavers. Like the skilled unemployed, the others had found that the demand for their labour had dropped with the onset of the recession: seventy-three per cent of the unemployed group had been made redundant at least once between 1979 and 1984. For the most part, however, they had not been made redundant from BSC. This confirms what we already know from the evidence of earlier chapters: the ex-steelworkers had some sort of advantage in the scramble for jobs after redundancy. Yet, although they may not have worked for BSC, we should not assume that the unemployed men in the sample were unacquainted with the steelworks. Half of them said they had worked for a BSC contractor.

## Who Were The Contracting Workers?
More than one in five of the sample had worked for a BSC contractor at some time over the previous ten years, however the men who had undertaken contracting work after Slimline in 1980 are of more interest. One in eight of the sample had worked for a

BSC contractor in their current job or, if they were now unemployed, had worked for a BSC contractor in their last job[2]. It is to this group that the analysis below refers, unless otherwise stated.

Before we can consider the way in which contracting workers were affected by downward social mobility, falling incomes and unemployment, it is necessary to point out that the contracting workers were not an homogeneous group. We know, from the previous chapter, that there were different types of contracting *work* and the same applies to the people who performed it. Some contracting workers may not have suffered quite as much as others from downward social mobility and so on. The most useful analysis is therefore one which begins by splitting up the contracting workers into sub-groups and then considers the type of contracting work performed by each of the sub-groups.

Using their previous work experience[3] the contracting workers could be split into three sub-groups. Firstly, there were people like Carl Roach and Peter Smith (see Chapter One), part of a heterogeneous group which had varied work experience — or none at all — but had never worked for BSC or for a contractor before 1980. This mixed group accounted for roughly two-fifths of the contracting workers. Secondly, just under a third of the contracting workers had, like three of the fitters we met in Chapter One, worked for BSC[4]. What kind of ex-BSC workers found jobs with contractors?

Some BSC workers interpreted the redundancies of 1980 as a signal that they should waste no time in abandoning a sinking ship. They wanted to get away from the steelworks altogether and were not interested in promises of work with contractors. These redundants, especially those who had been in more senior positions and, particularly, non-manual work, looked for jobs outside and looked early, If they were lucky enough they found work at the new Ford factory in Bridgend. Why did the redundants who went straight into contracting work not follow the same path?

> 'No other work and it was a job I knew.'
> 'Because the job was back down the harbour where I used to work.'
> 'Just needed a job and it was in The Works — contract for BSC.'

Obviously, the number of vacancies at Fords — or anywhere else outside 'The Works' — was limited, but familiarity was also important in these men's decision to 'settle' for contracting work. Although they were not amongst the *best*-placed to find work after redundancy, they were definitely not amongst the *worst*-placed redundants. It is also likely that these men were *told* (but not by the employers) that the contracting jobs would be long-term *before* they actually became redundant, or, at least, were not told otherwise. Whether because of false information, or because of the lack of alternatives, they tended to see the prospect of a contracting job as a good thing. They were asked about their expectations on being made redundant and some said they were hopeful of finding another job. They were asked why they were hopeful and their responses included the following:

' — — Engineering subcontract at BSC. Only (very hopeful) if they took on some redundant BSC electricians, myself being one.'
'Because I knew the contractor was taking over.'

Of course, the hopes of some of the redundants were not fulfilled:

'At the time I thought I would have had a job with contract cleaners.'
'There was a contract starting with another firm but I missed it.'

The *redundancy* survey provides some information on the factors which distinguished the redundants who were successful in finding jobs with the contractors (in the two years following their redundancy) from those who failed. Chapter Four showed that the redundants who found jobs with contractors were more likely to have worked in jobs or departments where contractors were brought in after 1980. The redundants who went to work for contractors were, of course, less likely to have had senior or non-manual jobs at BSC, but they were *more* likely to have had *general* manual skills. They were more likely to have been classified as 'semi-skilled' at BSC or to have had skills, like those of a fitter for example, which weren't specific to the jobs of steelworkers. Therefore, when at BSC, they were doing work which could easily be done by non-specialist outside firms. Furthermore, they could sell their *general* skills outside BSC, even if only to the contractors who took over. Thus forty per cent of the redundants who entered contracting work had these 'transferable skills' and they made up over a third of all those who had 'transferable skills' at BSC and had worked at some time after redundancy.

Finally, the survey of men in Port Talbot revealed a third group of men who had job histories like Frank Clark (see Chapter One) and might be called 'career contracting workers'. Twenty nine per cent of those who worked for a BSC contractor in their current or last job also did so between 1969 and 1978. Others said they had worked for a BSC contractor at some time in the last ten years as well as in their current or last job. In addition, there were men who had long experience of working for contracting firms, but not, until recently, firms which had contracts with BSC.

In order to explain what sort of work each of the sub-groups of contracting workers performed, it is as well to bear in mind that, *in general*, the best contracting jobs were with 'federated firms' (especially on 'nominated' projects where employers were most likely to observe national agreements) doing skilled work on a long contract (or, at least, regularly recurring short contracts).

The workers with the best overall chances of high pay and least spells out of work were the 'career contracting workers', especially those who were part of the elite of 'travelling men'. Nevertheless, falling demand throughout the contracting industry had reduced opportunities to remain in continuous employment by moving around the country and 'career contracting workers' in Port Talbot were increasingly forced to rely on work for contractors at BSC. They were, however, generally skilled, worked on nominated projects or at least for federated firms, and were the most likely to be asked to stay on to work on another project at the end of a contract. Next in the hierarchy were career contracting workers who had interrupted their spell with contractors with a period of employment at BSC. The latter proved something of a handicap after redundancy: they had been out of contracting work for a while and were possibly no longer members of the right union. They did, however, have a better chance of work with federated firms (and made up possibly ten per cent of these companies' workforces) than other ex-BSC workers who had no experience of contracting work. Hence the hope expressed by these BSC workers at the time of their redundancy. They were hopeful,

> 'Because I was prepared to spend a bit of time looking around and I worked with contractors before and could do that sort of job.'

If the job was to be with a federated firm, however, it is more than likely that there would be a delay between redundancy and the next spell of work. By way of contrast we have already seen that some ex-BSC workers went straight into contracting jobs. As the responses to the survey of BSC redundants showed, some found work because they came into contracting work straight from BSC:

> 'Had the option of staying with contractors.'
> 'Every five out, taking three on.'
> 'Already doing it, given to contractors.'
> 'It was my usual job'

These jobs were rarely with federated firms. Where work was transferred to a federated firm at the time of the redundancies, the employer would not recruit many ex-BSC workers because federated firms had their own sources of labour and saw little point in taking on BSC people for the sake of their make-up pay. They could not reduce wages to take advantage of make-up because they were party to agreements on pay with the trade unions. There was therefore no incentive to take on men who might be unskilled or have the wrong skills — although welders and boilermakers might be exceptions — or attitudes. In any event, the unions would have made it difficult for them to do so, if they had so wished, because ex-BSC people were usually in the wrong union.

Nevertheless, if you were a BSC redundant, but didn't have previous experience of work with contractors, you were more likely to get a 'good' contracting job if you got one straight after redundancy: if your job was simply transferred to a contractor you might continue to perform work of roughly the same level of skill. If you got into contracting late, however, it was likely to be as a cleaner or labourer and you were more likely to find work off-the-books. This also applied to the final group of contracting workers, those with no previous experience of work at BSC or with contractors.

### The Effects of Participation in Contracting Work

Whatever their experience before finding a job with a contractor, it is clear that contracting work must have had an effect on the contracting workers. Working for a contractor at BSC changed their status and produced several secondary effects.

Many contracting workers suffered downward social mobility: if we compare main occupation between 1969 and 1978 with occupation in current or last job, we find that the proportion of unskilled manual workers amongst the contracting group increased. Although they were more likely than the rest of the sample to have been in an unskilled occupation between 1969 and 1978, the gap between contracting workers and the others had increased significantly by the time of the survey. Not surprisingly, these men were well aware of their downward social mobility: when asked to compare their current or last job against others they had had, they were more likely than the rest of the sample to rate it as worse than most.

Contracting workers were downwardly mobile like the unemployed, *more so* in fact. Regression analysis of 1969-78 occupation against occupation in current or last job shows that there was less likelihood of the two being the same for the contracting workers than for any other group *including the unemployed* and of course more contracting workers went down (about twenty five per cent) than up. Contracting workers were *not* men who had started their working lives near the bottom of the ladder who had found they had to take the jobs nobody else wanted including, when things got tight, jobs with contractors. Instead, even more so than the unemployed, the men now classified as contracting workers were once considered skilled and their labour was once in demand. Although they were not highly *qualified* — three-quarters had no qualifications at all — a higher percentage of them had received apprentice training than the sample as a whole. They were also more likely to have had non-apprentice training, much of it on special schemes of one sort or another.

Participation in training schemes accounts for what little upward social mobility was found amongst the contracting workers. They had tried very hard to re-establish themselves — in view of falling demand for their labour — in occupations where it was easier to find employment either by acquiring skills where they had none, or by *re*training in order to acquire new skills. We know that at least one in four contracting workers was made redundant from BSC so we would expect that quite a few had — as had other ex-steelworkers — retrained. There was, as the case studies in Chapter One showed, considerable financial inducement for BSC redundants to enter training programmes. But the contracting workers' rate of participation in government schemes — the great majority of which were concerned with training — was *very* high: one in three as against nine per cent for the sample as a whole.

It is easy to see why *some* contracting workers might suffer downward social mobility: their new, contracting, occupations were simply lower down the occupational scale than their previous occupations *outside* contracting. But even the *career* contracting workers in the survey appeared to have dropped down the occupational hierarchy. In large part, these men had worked in metal goods and construction (and to a lesser extent in transport) in their main job between 1969 and 1978 and in their current or last job. In other words, they worked in precisely those industries where the contracting firms were concentrated. Career contracting workers worked in a variety of occupations in both metal goods and construction firms; however, in both industries their occupations in current or last job were generally ranked lower than in their 1969-78 job. This suggests that those career contracting workers who had not had much experience of contracting work *at BSC* before 1980 were forced down the occupational hierarchy by falling demand for their labour which left them no alternative but to work for firms with contracts at BSC[5]. At one time BSC contracting had been considered more attractive than other forms of contracting work but we have already seen (see Chapter Five) that there had been a change in the nature of contracting work at BSC over the years. After 1980 it was no longer the case that jobs with BSC contractors were specialised and highly skilled. With the expansion of contracting in the wake of Slimline, a number of much less desirable jobs had been put out to contractors and the career contractors took their share of these new contracting jobs with the rest (c.f. Danson, 1982).

Many contracting workers, but especially those who had slipped down the occupational hierarchy, had seen their incomes fall. In part this was because wages in contracting work had fallen, but contracting wages were in any case lower than in many of the workers' previous occupations (see Chapters One and Five). Nevertheless, the level of their incomes did not depend simply on wage rates.

Something like one in four of those men in the survey who were currently in contracting work had received make-up pay as BSC redundants. These men were less likely to be experienced in contracting work or to have skills relevant to contracting employment. They were therefore most likely to be hired by a contractor where their jobs were simply transferred directly from BSC so that they entered contracting immediately after redundancy. Of course the ease with which these redundants entered contracting work was, in large part, the result of BSC giving out contracts to non-federated firms. It was these companies which took over whole departments at BSC *and* paid wages low enough for their employees to claim make-up pay. Although their contracts might last for a year with the possibility of renewal, redundants who went to work for non-federated contractors were only better off than their colleagues in non-federated firms who were not ex-BSC workers as long as their make-up lasted (and they had much less chance of being shifted to another job by the same firm when the contract expired).

Since they were unemployed for much of the time, the incomes of the contracting workers also depended on the rate of welfare benefits. They were more likely than the sample as a whole to be reliant on supplementary benefit (the lowest rate of welfare payment) and less likely to receive non-wage income like interest or rent. In Chapter Five we discovered that contracting workers were more likely than the rest of the sample to be dissatisfied with their wage when in work. In the sample as a whole, respondents were more likely to say their pay had been good if they were now out of work. Since the contracting workers were more likely to have been unemployed at the time of the survey (see below), it is particularly surprising that they should have been dissatisfied with wages in their last jobs. This suggests that in some cases wages were so low that, even when compared to unemployment benefit or supplementary benefit, they did not seem attractive. Mainly as a result of their low and irregular incomes, the contracting workers were over-represented in the lowest household income bands. They were also less likely to own their own homes, or to have access to a relatively new car.

Participation in contracting work resulted in downward social mobility, falling incomes and, finally, periodic unemployment[6]. The group of contracting workers we have been discussing in this chapter consisted of men who were either working for a BSC contractor at the time of the interview *or* were unemployed at the time of the interview but had worked for a BSC contractor in their *last* job. In fact twenty two of the thirty eight men in the group fell into the latter category. That is, fifty-eight per cent of the contracting workers were not in work (as opposed to thirty-eight per cent of the rest of the sample). Of the twenty two contracting workers who were not in work, only four had 'withdrawn' from the labour market. This meant that forty seven per cent of the contracting workers were *unemployed and available for work* (as against sixteen per cent of the rest of the sample).

The thirty eight men who were classified as contracting workers were not the only men in the survey to have some experience of contracting work. Earlier in this chapter we learnt that over a fifth of the sample had worked for a BSC contractor *at some time* in the previous ten years. Of these sixty four men, twenty five were unemployed when they were interviewed and a further eight had 'withdrawn' from the labour market. This left only thirty one in work, that is only forty-eight per cent of the men with contracting experience were working whereas sixty-four per cent of the men without contracting experience were in work. The men with contracting experience were three times as likely as the others to be living on supplementary benefit and four times as likely to be receiving unemployment benefit. Because the contracting workers were so vulnerable to unemployment, they made up nearly half of *all* the men who were unemployed and available for work.

By coincidence the same number, sixty four, of workers with experience of contracting work turned up in the survey of the workers made redundant by BSC. The majority had had two or more spells of unemployment since their redundancy two years before and over a third were unemployed and available for work at the time of the interview. Furthermore, a majority (thirty four) had had at least four 'statuses' (a job, unemployment, or retraining) after redundancy. (Two men actually had ten or more statuses). Most of the sixty four had had at least two jobs since redundancy and eleven had four or more jobs. A quarter of the group's completed spells of employment had lasted less than two months and sixty per cent of these spells had lasted less than four months. Only twenty three men had had a job lasting for more than twelve months since being made redundant by BSC. Similarly, contracting workers in the Port Talbot survey were more likely than the others to say that their longest period of employment in the previous five years had lasted less than twelve months.

Both the redundancy survey and the Port Talbot survey show that contracting workers experienced short spells of work interspersed with short spells of unemployment. For a minority, however, the short spell of work was followed by a much longer period of unemployment. I asked the area manager of a contracting firm what happened to his workers when a job ended:

> 'Normally, in the past, a gang of men who worked on contracting, if they weren't continuously employed (say they were one of the last ones in on a contract) would be picked up by another contractor and do the rounds between firms. But these days because of the shortage of work, it usually means they are laid off. We were surprised the other day when enquiring about a bloke we'd had twelve or eighteen months ago and they said, "He's been laid off since he worked for you eighteen months ago".'

An employers' representative agreed: contracting workers who were paid off went on the dole and looked for work with other contractors and perhaps did off-the-books work or other undeclared work on their own account (both of these types of work are included in the general local term 'hobble'). In contrast to the 1970s, when trade was 'good all over' many now stayed on the dole; 'there are lots of unemployables anyway'. Peter Smith was presumably one of the 'unemployables' (even though he was trained as a fitter and willing to work long hours at short notice for £2 an hour). When I last interviewed Peter he had given up hope of getting back to work with the contractor at BSC. He and his wife seemed to be preparing for a long spell on supplementary benefit — in fact, they had just had some money from the DHSS to allow them to buy carpets to put on the bare boards of their flat and to buy an insulation jacket for their hot-water heater. This would help them to cut down on heating costs now the weather was not so good.

**Footnotes**

1. The proportion of the unemployed who were classified as 'social class' III (skilled manual) is much higher than we might have expected and goes some way towards explaining why only sixty per cent of this class were in a full-time job. Nevertheless, respondents to the survey were more likely to be *available* for work if they were classified as semi-skilled or unskilled, and more than half of the unemployed men in III (skilled manual) had actually withdrawn from the labour market. Note that only forty-two per cent of 'social class' IV and forty-six per cent of 'social class' V were in work at the time of the survey. Thirty per cent of all 'social classes' IV and V were unemployed *and available for work*.
2. But note that only half of these men were actually on the BSC site all the time.
3. Some of my colleagues at University College of Swansea thought that the question of who the contracting workers were ought to be answered in another way, by using a classification based on the 'social networks' described in the

previous chapter. If people had different types or sizes of 'networks' might this not explain why some people ended up in contracting jobs and others did not (and stayed on the dole but possibly with the chance, ultimately, of a better job but not with a contractor)?

On a fairly simplistic level, if the people who get contracting jobs have larger 'social networks' one would expect them to be more 'sociable', and this was *not* one of the findings of the Port Talbot Survey. Firstly, the contracting workers were no more likely than others to be members of a leisure or sports club or of the other local societies where people in the town might meet. Secondly, the contracting workers were no more likely to be involved in the affairs of a church or chapel. In fact, the survey showed that most of the socialising in Port Talbot went on in 'social clubs' ('workingmen's clubs'), yet contracting workers were no more likely than the others in the sample to be members of these clubs (you did not really have to be a member to attend however), *with two exceptions.* The exceptions were two social clubs on the Sandfields estate, and it is worth noting that the contracting workers were no more likely to live on the estate than anyone else. In both cases well over a third of the sampled members of these clubs were contracting workers. Furthermore, the contracting workers in the survey made more use of the social clubs in the town than did the rest of the sample: they were more likely to have been to a club in the last twenty four hours and to have been there more frequently than the rest during the preceding month, and a few contracting workers were members of social club committees. Yet if the contracting workers *are* more sociable, who did they see when they were socialising: was it people who could help them to find work?

The survey showed that contracting workers were more likely than the rest to know people who worked for one of the large local contractors, but we would expect something like this since these men may have worked for that firm themselves and the statistical association was, in any case, not all that strong. In fact fieldwork amongst the contracting workers did not suggest a 'closely knit network' in which all the men knew each other. Furthermore, the Port Talbot survey did not suggest they lived together as neighbours in certain parts of the town: there was no evidence that they were 'clustered' in particular areas. Nevertheless, we know that, in at least two social clubs, the contracting workers had the opportunity to drink together. But what good was this — surely they were all in the same boat? Peter Smith provided the answer: if all of your mates are looking for work then you can cover a much wider area than one person could on his own. In fact the only group which the contracting workers had more contact with (than the rest of the sample) was the *unemployed*!

My colleagues at Swansea concluded that, *when unemployment rises*, a worker's access to informal means of finding work may increase his or her chances of getting a job. This may well be true but we should not overplay the point. Lots of people in Port Talbot had access to informal means of finding work, but it was those who found jobs with contracting firms who made most use of this access. It is not at all clear that the contracting workers had, for example, different 'social networks' or larger 'social networks' when compared with the longer-term unemployed, and it may be that other factors (such as those described in this chapter) were more important in deciding which unemployed men got the occasional job with a contractor and which remained permanently out of work. In any event the fact that 'networks' can carry information about *applicants* as well as jobs may turn out to be the most important aspect of the informal way in which contracting jobs are filled (see Chapter Five).

4. Although the contracting workers did not, in the main, work for BSC either in their main occupation between 1969 and 1978 or in their current or last job, they were more likely than the sample as a whole to have been *made redundant* by BSC.

5. Alternatively, the *firms* these men worked for were forced to go for BSC contracts because of the lack of other work.

6. According to the local job centre, when the contracts for the installation of Concast at Port Talbot were completed in 1982 Port Talbot's unemployment figures received their biggest single boost in the whole period 1980-82, except, of course, for the BSC redundancies. The unemployment figures received similar — although smaller — boosts every time a contract for BSC ended.

# Chapter Seven

# The Trade Unions And The Legacy of Slimline

According to Kevin Morgan the leadership of the Conservative Party had decided *before* the 1979 general election, that they could pick a fight with the steel unions and win. Because of their internal fragmentation the steel unions were amongst the weakest of trade union opponents a future Conservative government would face (Morgan, 1983: 189). This proved to be the case in practice: BSC's programme of restructuring was 'facilitated by the traditions and fragmentation of the steel unions' (Morgan, 1983: 175).

The extent of the traditional divisions within and between the steel unions is documented by Morgan and by Martin Upham (1980), and there is no need to repeat the analysis here. It may be useful, however, to repeat some of the things which Morgan says about the largest steel union, ISTC. Morgan calls ISTC a 'company union', one of the 'most authoritarian in Britain', (it has only had a consultative national conference since 1976). He says that ISTC is renowned for its 'conservative' and 'highly fragmented membership base', and for its rivalry with the craft unions. Finally, ISTC is 'remarkable' for the lack of communication between its constituent regions: the steelworks of Port Talbot and Llanwern, for example, were in separate divisions of ISTC (Morgan, 1983: 190-3).

Chapter Two showed how the events of 1980 left the steel unions — including ISTC — in total disarray. This chapter will show how ill-equipped the trade unions were to deal with the new challenges that faced them *after* Slimline as BSC brought in contractors to do the work of BSC employees. It deals with two areas of union activity: their dealings with BSC, and their dealings with the contracting firms themselves.

### The Unions and BSC

In 1980 the union officials at BSC Port Talbot who had accepted Slimline were required to secure their *members*' acceptance of the agreement. In this process they used the contractors element of the Slimline package as a *selling point*. Firstly, they could point to the fact that many of the jobs which were to go out to contract were the least desirable in the works and imply that nobody would mourn their passing into the hands of outside contractors. Take, for example, the work of heavy cleaners: one of the regular tasks performed by the cleaning gangs involved using water sprays to clean off oxide deposits in the strip mills each week. The deposits were washed into pits below the mill and grabbed out as 'scale' (some of which was recycled). Other cleaning jobs in the mills included cleaning out the sprays which kept the hot (strip) steel cool, and emptying out oil pits. As Derek Rees said,

> 'The men who've been in the mill all their lives would be keen to relinquish *these* jobs if they had to.'

Other jobs which were earmarked for the contractors were just as dirty and unpopular, for example shovelling up graphite dust before the cranes could start work each morning, cleaning up spillage amidst the fumes of the BOS plant, and cleaning up acid spillage on the pickle line.

The second selling point of BSC's proposals for contractors, as far as the unions were concerned, apparently contradicts the first. But whereas the point about dirty jobs applied in a general way to all the workers in the plant, the second selling point only applied to those workers who might expect to be made redundant. These people could be told that BSC's plans represented a good deal for them, personally. They would have enviable severance terms and other allowances *and* could soon expect to be back in the steelworks, perhaps in their old jobs, as the employees of contractors. As one of the redundants explained, the unions told them not to worry, they would make sure the contractors took on people who had been made redundant. The only problem, he continued, was that the redundants didn't realise at what cost their cooperation was being bought because they had no idea what sort of wages and conditions the contractors would offer them.

In time it became clear that workers throughout BSC had 'fallen for' the promise of employment with contractors after redundancy. In 1983/4 the TUC Steel Committee heard a string of similar complaints from the unions. Thus a divisional officer of ISTC in Scotland wrote:

> 'Firstly, because the jobs put to contract have been non mainstream production jobs there have been more than enough volunteers, cross-matching, etc. Our ability to fight this form of privatisation has therefore been reduced to Nil. On the basis of not fighting losers therefore we have become increasingly reluctant to oppose such proposals when we are aware that both officials and members desire that particular route.'

In January 1984 the Steel Committee discussed BSC's increased use of contractors and

> '...reference was again made to the great difficulties created for unions in their attempts to oppose this practice by the terms which BSC offered

workers to transfer from direct BSC employment to contractors'
employment. These had the appearance of being very advantageous to
individuals in cash terms, and for many workers this outweighed the
loss of all the non-wage benefits which the Committee had negotiated
over the years.'

The immediate legacy of Slimline put local union officials at Port
Talbot in an unenviable position. Because they had 'agreed' to
Slimline and had to sell the deal to their members, they were forced
to give the appearance of being happy to see some jobs transferred
from BSC to contractors. In subsequent months, however, the
union officials' position might have improved. There were three
reasons to expect that things might have been different after
Slimline. Firstly, the officials had more opportunity to resist BSC's
use of contractors. Secondly, their leaders were opposed to the use
of contractors. Thirdly, their members were increasingly hostile to
the use of contractors. We will deal with each of these points in turn.

After Slimline, proposals to bring in contractors were no longer
part of a non-negotiable package. In the years after 1980 such
proposals were made either as 'one-off' localised proposals in a
particular department, or as more general proposals linked to the
annual plant-wide *Lump Sum Bonus Scheme* negotiations. Since
the move away from national to local negotiations in BSC,
confirmed by a national deal struck in 1980, annual plant-level
negotiations over the Lump Sum Bonus Scheme had become the
focus for discussions about 'manning' levels and, therefore,
discussions about management proposals to bring in contractors. At
these negotiations increases in earnings — through bonus payments
— were tied to further reductions in employment which might be
facilitated by changes in working practices or by putting work out to
contract.

Local trade union officials therefore had more *opportunity* to
resist BSC's proposals to bring in contractors after 1980, but did
they have more *need* to resist? The head offices of the steel unions
had, by this time, woken up to the fact that BSC's use of contractors
amounted to privatisation. Further inactivity threatened to prove
embarrassing, particularly at the TUC where other unions — for
example those in the health service and in telecommunications —
were putting up more vigorous opposition to privatisation. It was
therefore to be expected that pressure from the head offices of the
steel unions on local union officials would be increased. In the event
this pressure amounted to very little. Some regional officers were
very concerned about BSC's use of contractors but they had no
direct influence over the lay officials in their areas. Trade union
leaders, moreover, did not appear anxious to take the initiative.
Shortly after they learnt of the full extent of BSC's increased use of

contractors during 1980, members of the TUC Steel Committee suggested that

'it would be futile to attempt to oppose the development, especially as it was manifestly more economical for BSC to employ contractors in certain roles.'

The Committee however agreed that they should raise the matter with BSC and that their

'...policy should remain one of opposing the unnecessary use of contractors and encouraging the negotiation by the membership at works' level of adequately protective agreements...'

It is clear from subsequent deliberations of the Steel Committee that their policy of opposition to the use of contractors had little real effect. Even in 1984 the Committee were no more confident of their ability to deliver the goods:

'in the circumstances which have existed for several years now, the committee have been unable to effectively prevent the extension of sub-contracting. Moreover, there is the problem of how many members have shown themselves ready to accept redundancy from BSC (and redundancy pay) with the promise of getting a very similar job with a contractor to the one they were doing in the Corporation, and sometimes almost at once. It is unlikely that further approaches to BSC, at this stage, will have any more success than have recent ones in persuading the Corporation to change, and, indeed to reverse its policy on this matter.'

The trade union leaders were, however, wrong to think that all their members were happy to see more jobs go out to contractors. BSC workers were increasingly hostile to BSC's use of contractors. Hostility was even expressed by BSC workers who were not *directly* threatened, that is workers whose jobs would not be lost if a specific proposal to contract out work was accepted. (In part this may have been because they feared that poor quality work by contractors would affect the productivity bonus paid to all BSC employees). I reported at an early stage in the research that their resistance included refusals to work with contractors' employees, to lend them tools or even the kettle to make tea. Of course, the contractors' employees were sometimes in a position to retaliate — for example, when installing new machinery they did not always feel obliged to explain its intricacies to BSC workers.

Trade union officials at Llanwern near Newport claimed that there was now less hostility between BSC workers — at least for those not involved in maintenance work — and the employees of contracting firms 'because people understand it more', that is union officials had persuaded some BSC workers that contracting out work might not be a bad thing. Nevertheless, Llanwern officials advised BSC to keep contracting workers away from areas of the plant where BSC employees were at work, in order to avoid hostility which arose because:

> 'that sort of "I could be on the road next", not-seeing-the-wider-picture, philosophy is still there.'

It should be clear by now that local union officials — at least in theory — were in a stronger position to resist further increases in the use of contractors after the dust from Slimline had settled. How did they respond? Local union officials at Port Talbot responded (eventually) by setting up a Contractors' Committee. One ISTC full-timer said that it was not until 'years' after Slimline that this Committee 'started to function properly', however even then the Committee was hardly a roaring success.

The Contractors' Committee at Port Talbot was set up as a sub-committee of the top-level multi-union committee (later the 'Slimline Committee') and was staffed by senior members of this committee. One of them explained the Committee's aims to me. Firstly, the Committee should make sure that contracting workers were in the appropriate union and, secondly, the Committee should monitor any proposals to bring in more contractors. The problems of organising the contracting workers will be considered in the next section. Here we will deal only with the Committee's second aim.

The Committee member I talked to admitted that, for most of the time, this aim was not achieved. When it came to fighting a proposal to bring in contractors, he said, the Committee were hampered by a lack of information (similar complaints were made by union officials at other BSC plants, for example at Workington). They simply did not know when such a proposal had been made, and when they did find out it was too late for the Contractors' Committee to do anything about it. Line management were not communicating, for example not always informing the shop steward of a proposal to bring in contractors. The steward responsible for the affected department *should* have had the chance to argue that BSC employees could do the work instead, either within normal working hours or in overtime. If the steward had made a case for direct labour, s/he should then take the costings to the relevant union convenor.

It might be thought that union officials at Port Talbot were accustomed to expect too much of their shop stewards, however Committee members complained that even where they did have advance information about a proposal to bring in contractors they were handicapped by a lack of information on the *cost* of the proposal. They could not query the proposal on a cost-basis because

BSC would not tell them how much they would pay the contractors. The senior member of the Contractors' Committee also told me that when they did get information on costs, after the event, BSC managers told the unions they had done their sums wrong[1]. 'Every month' the unions heard of cases where work had been put out to contractors and yet BSC had not saved money. They would have heard of more cases but stewards or members did not always inform their convenor. When they took these examples to BSC they were told their calculations were mistaken, usually because they had assumed contracting employees would be working normal hours on a fixed-price job (often they would in fact be working longer hours hence reducing the hourly rate paid by the contractor).

Despite all the obstacles that they felt BSC had put in their way, the Port Talbot officials said there was a point beyond which they would not be pushed. This was why they were prepared to make such a fuss — they intended to work normally and force BSC to lock them out — over BSC's proposal to bring contractors into packing in the cold mill. They thought this proposal was an important development because it would mean bringing in contractors to do 'traditional steelworkers' jobs'. One of the full-timers involved in the packing dispute explained this in a letter to union leaders:

'Although we have averted what could have been a very nasty situation, the problem will not run away, and we need to make our total opposition to the use of contractors on production jobs clear to the Corporation.'

'This was a significant step by the Corporation, to extend the use of Contractors. In the past they have argued that catering, cleaning, etc. are not in their line of business, and other people could do it more efficiently, or they do not have enough work to warrant running their own department. However, here we had a proposal to put regular production work out to contract. I feel we must tell the Corporation we are not going to allow this to happen, or there will be no end to how far they would extend the principle.'

There are two points to note here. Firstly the line beyond which BSC could not go was more frequently drawn by full-timers than lay officials[2]. Secondly, the line drawn by the unions was a very wavy one indeed.

An ISTC full-timer said there was now no doubt about the unions' determination to keep contractors out of 'steelworkers jobs': people had been kicked out of office for flouting this policy and they knew that they would be kicked out for good if it happened again. Full-timers would reverse any case where head office policy had not been observed, and all the negotiating committees and union branches were now aware that they could not go against their unions. But was head office policy as clear as this implies? I found

that the meaning of 'production job' was still not precise and that
the policy was difficult to put into practice if taken too literally. In
fact the officials at Port Talbot used it flexibly to describe any job
that they didn't want to lose to contractors. Something similar
might be said of the full-timers' argument.

I asked one of the ISTC full-timers to explain how a
'steelworker's job' could be recognised. He said that BSC managers
at both Port Talbot and Llanwern had gone just about as far as they
could in putting work out to contractors because his union would
not allow them to bring contractors into *production*, that is the
production jobs involved in everything from coke making to sheet
steel finishing. This was a 'fall back position' reached after the
unions had submitted when the 'politics of fear' reigned during and
after 1980.

In sum, the unions were only *able* to put up a fight when all but
production jobs had been put out to contractors. Furthermore,
where there was effective trade union resistance, the unions'
'victories' were usually hollow. Thus one of the few really
concerned full-time officers — not an ISTC officer — related the
story of BSC's attempt to introduce contractors into packing in the
cold mill in September 1983. This proposal affected both the
members of this man's union and ISTC members. He told how his
union had had to 'fight' the ordinary membership in order to
persuade them to resist the proposal. The members knew they
would receive augmented severance payments and would have a
good chance of going straight back into employment with the
contractors since these firms would need people who were familiar
with the work.

The union officer went to the relevant branch meeting and told
the members that this was the thin end of the wedge and that the
jobs of other branch members could be on the line next. He was
successful and was actually able to use his success to put pressure on
union leaders by making them aware of the 'strength' of local
opposition to the use of contractors. This had little effect, however,
and he felt that, in the end, BSC 'won their point' because of the
changes the unions had to make in order to keep the contractors
out. Officials of the ISTC did not see it this way, however. The
senior ISTC official involved in this case told me that productivity
had been low in packing anyway, he had been warning the members
about it for years, and low productivity meant that there was no
guarantee of long-term security for the workers in that part of the
cold mill. The ISTC branch official who was directly responsible for
those workers explained that they had made direct labour cheaper
in order to persuade BSC not to bring in contractors, by cutting
down materials waste and by eliminating some job demarcation. He

made no mention of the job losses which the unions had accepted yet, according to the officer of the other union involved, these workers had taken a pay cut and reduced employment from 42 to 28 in order to match BSC's figures. This saved a total of £350,000 in the first year of operation of the new arrangements.

When there was effective trade union resistance to the use of contractors, it seems that union members in BSC suffered from the ensuing compromise required to keep the contractors out. But *why* were the unions only able to mount a semblance of resistance when BSC threatened to put production jobs out to contractors? While the 'politics of fear' were the *immediate* legacy of Slimline, Slimline also had longer-term effects on the unions.

At the end of Chapter Two I explained how Slimline created divisions and distrust which handicapped the unions in subsequent years. There were, firstly, divisions *between union members*, divisions which were made to tell by BSC's strategy, especially the strategy employed at annual negotiations over the Lump Sum Bonus Scheme.

A full-time officer of one of the craft unions at BSC explained that the usual sequence of events — something which had occurred on 'numerous occasions' — was that BSC would propose an increase in their use of contractors in a particular area and the union would fight the proposal where they felt management was most vulnerable. For example, the unions would 'catch them on the pickle line' or at another point in the production process where BSC could not afford a strike because all output would be affected. BSC would then give way but, at the next annual negotiations, the proposal to introduce contractors could be reintroduced[3]. Management would ensure that the major departments in the works were not affected by the proposal and the majority of the workforce would then accept an increase in the use of contractors on behalf of the minority who were directly affected.

In sum, it seems that the workers' best chance of resisting management initiatives over contractors was to restrict the fight so that only those workers who were to be affected directly would be involved. This could be done with a 'one-off' proposal to bring in contractors but not at the Lump Sum Bonus Scheme negotiations. One of the ISTC officials involved in these negotiations confirmed this was the case: the unions were far more likely to be successful where the battle was fought by small groups of workers, individual union branches, or even the individual negotiating committees for staff, for workers in heavy steel and workers in finishing. The official could only think of one case where the battle was won by the plant's multi-union committee[4]. Yet even where a relatively small number of workers was involved the problem of the minority accepting on behalf of the majority remained (as in the cold mill packing dispute).

But were the members always the source of the difficulty? Union officials at BSC Llanwern claimed, for example, that officials at Port Talbot *fostered* dissension between members. For instance, they believed that the unions at Port Talbot had 'bought off' some members by giving them overtime where management wanted to introduce contractors. Thus management would inform a local official of its intention to bring in contractors but would offer increased overtime for those workers who remained. The union official would then use this offer of overtime to buy the acceptance of his members. This was, the Llanwern officials claimed, why Port Talbot and (at an earlier stage) Ravenscraig, had both excessive overtime for BSC employees and excessive numbers of contracting workers[5].

ISTC officials at Port Talbot admitted that the craft unions — with smaller numbers and less divisions between members — had been more successful in resisting BSC's proposals to bring in contractors after 1980, and there had been cases where craft unions had resisted successfully and had not lost jobs in the process. ISTC was originally a confederation of the steel unions and it grew by gradually taking over groups of workers who were involved in very different areas of work. Divisions between these union members remained and are still formally recognised in the union's branch structures and negotiating practices. There has always been some potential for groups of workers who are still seen as 'peripheral' to the union to be abandoned. This might sound a rather harsh term, but let's look at ISTC's attitude towards bringing in contractors before 1980. BSC's use of contractors did something to keep ISTC members amongst the elite of manual workers before 1980: at one time members 'didn't touch' certain jobs, even if short-term pay might be higher, and they told management which jobs they *would* do. We might think that the unions accepted contractors *during* 1980 because they had no alternative, but this was certainly not the case either before, or after, 1980. It might be concluded that BSC's increased use of contractors in subsequent years actually suited at least one of the trade unions affected, at any rate the peculiar attitude of ISTC officials did not endear them to the members of other unions. For one thing, some of the 'peripheral' — for example, non-production — jobs which ISTC officials were prepared to lose were in fact the jobs of members of other unions.

Secondly, resistance to BSC's increased use of contractors was hampered by divisions between local officials and head offices. Trade union leaders complained that the local officials' acquiescence in 1980 had left the leadership with no basis on which to fight further increases in the use of contractors. A TUC Steel Committee office paper explained that

> 'Some, perhaps all, recent Slimline, and similar, agreements appear to concede BSC the right to use contractors ... (eg) the 1980 Llanwern Agreement: "... The management continues to reserve the right to use contractors on work of either a regular or irregular nature ..."
>
> 'The Committee will therefore wish to be on guard against a repetition of the challenge which the Corporation have issued in the recent past, to the effect that the Committee are opposing at a national level what their members have accepted, for survival, at a local level.'

In similar vein, trade union leaders blamed local negotiations over the Lump Sum Bonus Scheme for their inability to resist, effectively, BSC's proposals to bring in contractors. They claimed their opposition would be ineffective because local officials had already agreed to accept such proposals when they signed their own local agreements. In fact concern was regularly expressed by lay members at ISTC conferences about these local negotiations. These union officials would have preferred to have all negotiations of this kind conducted centrally. (Unlike other unions, ISTC had no full-time officers at these negotiations). Local agreements gave BSC too much power and allowed them (as we have already seen) to play off one branch against another. In the face of such complaints, ISTC leaders were adamant that local agreements would remain; and it was of course these very leaders who had orchestrated the shift from centrally conducted negotiations in 1980.

*The Unions and the Contractors*
In Chapter Five we learnt that the unions concerned with the contractors had to accept the renegotiation of a national agreement on the employers' terms but we also learnt that the unions were now too weak to force all the employers to subscribe to an agreement which favoured management because some firms no longer felt it necessary to be members of the employers' organisation. Of course, even where employers were party to a national agreement through their membership of the employers' organisation, the responsibility for operating that agreement was in the hands of the local union organisation. The agreement counted for little if the workforce was not unionised and the local organisation was too weak to persuade local employers to stand by the agreement reached with their representatives. The unions faced difficulties in three key areas: in recruiting members in contracting firms, in monitoring wages and conditions, and in negotiating over wages and conditions.

Trade unions must recruit members before they can improve their wages and conditions, but it seems that the steel unions could not clear this first hurdle (a problem they shared with some other

British unions, *Guardian*, 21 January 1987). Of course, this could be, at least in part, because of the temporary nature of work with contractors. A new recruiting effort was required every time the contract was put out to tender. But it could also be that the unions were primarily, perhaps solely, interested in swelling the paper membership and not in improving their (new) members' wages and conditions. Thus ISTC sources said that BSC's increased use of contractors had contributed to an overall drop in membership because wherever a process had been put out to tender the number of workers had fallen.

In 1981 the TUC Steel Committee resolved to take positive steps towards organising the contracting workers. In the process they agreed the following principle which would be applied in cases of *inter-union disputes* over members in contracting firms:

> 'where BSC employs contractors to undertake work of a kind for which a particular union already holds the membership and negotiating rights, then that union should retain those rights'.

The Steel Committee's agreement about which unions should organise contractors' employees was difficult to put into practice, although more difficult in some regions than others. Differences between regions arose because the pattern of trade union organisation *before* contractors were brought in — which unions organised which parts of a plant — varied from region to region. ISTC might, for example, 'lose' workers to the TGWU when work went out to contract in one part of the country; but workers doing the same jobs would already have been TGWU members, when working for BSC, in another part of the country. In Wales it seems that the former case was more usual: ISTC full-timers felt their union was disadvantaged by the Steel Committee's agreement, and there were a number of wrangles between the ISTC and (in fact) the TGWU about which union should organise contractors' employees. At one stage the TGWU accused ISTC of poaching their members in a particular contracting firm at work at BSC Port Talbot and later demanded that ISTC repay the union dues they had collected to the TGWU.

One of the ISTC's full-time officers in Wales thought that the ISTC officials at BSC Port Talbot had been particularly remiss in organising the employees of contracting firms. Whereas at Llanwern the local union officials had involved their full-time regional officers from the very start of the (Slimline) reductions in direct employment in 1980, the Port Talbot officials had deliberately excluded the regional officers from any discussions. When BSC management at Llanwern wanted to increase their use of contractors the full-timers were able to ask management for a schedule in advance (although the *most* advanced warning came through 'unofficial' channels), and set about organising the contracting firms' workers when — or before — they came on site.

At Port Talbot, however, the local officials were unable to rely on their full-timers for help. The officers said simply that if the Port Talbot branches thought they could manage on their own when reductions in employment were being discussed they could rely on their own resources to organise the contractors. The ISTC full-timer claimed that his union therefore had a smaller proportion of potential members at Port Talbot than Llanwern as a result. The contractors' employers at Port Talbot were either unorganised or 'in the wrong union'. Nevertheless, the position had improved recently because the full-timers were now involved at Port Talbot and because BSC was now more forthcoming about its proposals to further extend the use of contractors there. Not surprisingly, the local union officials at Port Talbot emphasised this latter point and said nothing about their rift with the full-time officers.

Earlier in this chapter we discovered that the Contractors' Committee at Port Talbot had two aims: to *monitor* the increased use of contractors and to *organise* the contractors' employees. A senior member of this Committee told me that for some time they were unable to achieve the second aim because management were slow to give them the necessary information, for example, details of which contractors would be coming on site. In theory every worker coming onto the site should have been a union member (although the unions did not even *try* to ensure that this was the case for workers who were only on site for a short time) but every month the Committee recorded cases where this did not happen. When challenged, management explained that these cases were the fault of *sub*-contractors, over whom they had no control. The Contractors' Committee, however, thought the cause was the same as in their difficulties over monitoring:

> 'The Committee is knackered at all times because BSC line management is not communicating.'

BSC had made some efforts, by sending out a letter to line management informing them of the proper procedure for letting the unions know where contracts of a week or more are given out, to improve the situation:

> 'But even today the Committee constantly say they're having the same problem. It's in the minutes every month.'

With the result that:

> 'it's very difficult for the Committee members to keep tabs and they need the shop floor to keep an eye out.'

As a non-partisan source close to the unions commented, this put a lot of pressure on the union shop stewards, who

> 'have to have eyes in the backs of their heads, have to be on the look out for a stranger.'

Because contractors were appearing all over the works, the stewards did not know where a strange face might pop up next.

Concern over the size of a union's membership can lead its representatives into some contradictory and anomalous practices.Before we go on to investigate the union's negotiations with contractors over pay and conditions, consider the following situation. Other unions have pointed out that, if ISTC members were displacing members of other unions as employees of contractors because their access to make-up pay allowed them to accept lower wages, then low wages amongst the contracting firms were actually a *good thing* from ISTC's point of view. ISTC officers admitted that their members did 'jump the queue' for some jobs with contractors, but asked what they were supposed to do about it? On the other hand, ISTC officers were involved in negotiations with the EEC to introduce a minimum wage in the contracting firms without which make-up would not be paid, in order to end the abuse of make-up pay. Yet even if this scheme were successful, the unions cannot be absolved of responsibility for low wages amongst contractors.

Because the unions had been less than reluctant to see the least popular jobs go out to contractors, contracting workers were already likely to number amongst the low-paid. Yet the wages paid by contractors were generally even lower than the wages BSC had paid when the work was done in-house (see Chapter Five). The obvious way for the steel unions to influence contracting workers' wages and conditions was through the agency of BSC itself. Thus one union officer told union leaders that they should:

> 'Tell the corporation we are totally opposed to the use of contractors on production *and* they should set out minimum rates of pay and holiday entitlement in the contracts they put out to tender.'

Indeed, it appears that at some BSC plants the unions were able to achieve this aim. It was reported to the TUC Steel Committee early in 1984 that trade unions at Scunthorpe had been able to negotiate a 'no worse conditions' agreement. However, a senior ISTC officer later claimed that this agreement — that contracting workers should be no worse off than when the work was done by BSC employees — had later broken down. Unions in the North East of England had also pressed BSC on this issue, although the resulting agreement was less clearcut. The 'BSC Teesside Agreement — Use of

Contractors' included the following clause:

> 'All contractors employed should have up to date membership of a trade union appropriate to the work being carried out as defined by national/local agreements and practices and must satisfy BSC of their employment conditions and union membership arrangements.'

Nevertheless, the Steel Committee was informed that the 'safeguard amounted to nothing' because BSC was refusing to increase its payments to the contractors.

Port Talbot's union officials never won an agreement which BSC could dishonour, but they also complained that BSC was the source of their difficulties when trying to improve contractors' wages and conditions. In this they were not alone. Almost all trade union sources said that contractors throughout the UK were unable to increase wages because BSC would not let them. In Scotland, for example:

> '...pressure exerted by BSC on contractors to cut their tender prices to the bone is a contributory factor in the contractors' payment of low wages. Where men resist the low wages, the contractor concerned loses the job, as his tender price, reflecting the higher wage content, is too high.'

As well as in South Wales: ISTC officials at Ebbw Vale complained that

> 'If contracts change hands following acceptance by BSC of a lower tender, we are left with:
>
> (a) Redundancies — with inevitably no redundancy payments.
> (b) Dealings with new contractors regarding recognition rights, etc.
> (c) Possible lower rate of pay.
> (d) Invariably less employed.
> (e) No protection under E.P.A. [Employment Protection Act].'

In one case in 1983 an Ebbw Vale official had been forced to accept a two and a half per cent cent increase in wages for low-paid contractors' employees because BSC would not allow the firm to increase its prices. Even at Llanwern the union officials had little leverage in negotiations with contractors. Nowadays the employers told the unions what BSC had said they could put on the table as a wage increase. The situation in all the BSC plants was neatly summarised by an ISTC official from Ebbw Vale:

> 'We cannot "genuinely" negotiate with the contractor as it is the BSC who hold the purse strings.'

I asked one of the ISTC full-timers for Wales to describe in detail how negotiations with contractors at Llanwern and Port Talbot had changed in character over the years. He said that in the old days, at

Llanwern at least, they were used to dealing with 'contractors who were there all the time.' They would send these firms a copy of the national agreement made between ISTC and BSC. The contractor would then go back to BSC and the Corporation would look at the contractors' employment costs to ascertain whether an increase in the contract price was justified by the national agreement (which nominally only applied to BSC workers of course). If they were satisfied that it did, then BSC would fund the required increase in wages by allowing the contractors to increase their prices accordingly. This practice ceased in 1980 with the Slimline Agreement and was replaced by a 'cut-throat situation' in which BSC no longer made money available for contractors' wage increases. At Port Talbot *and* Llanwern BSC now wanted the cheapest contractor available and this meant a 'hell of a job for the divisional officers.' If officers complained to BSC about the new policy, the management said that the contractors' wages had 'nothing to do with them'. Nevertheless, although BSC's response was the same at both Port Talbot and Llanwern, the situation at Port Talbot was appreciably worse.

The ISTC full-timer reported that at Port Talbot a contractor had ordered an ISTC officer out of his office — 'that would never happen at Llanwern' — and the legacy of earlier rifts between full-timers and local union officials led to difficulties after union officers tried to negotiate with any contractor at Port Talbot. In part, these difficulties arose because the full-timers received information about work going out to contract at Port Talbot too late, but there were other difficulties. Thus the full-timer related the story of his negotiations with a particular Port Talbot contractor, one which a senior trade union official at Port Talbot referred to as 'that bloody firm'. I shall call the bloody firm 'Contract Cleaners Ltd.'

Early in 1983 the ISTC full-timer was called in by a branch official to negotiate with 'Contract Cleaners.' The firm told him that they could not meet the union's claims for increased wages and longer holidays *and* wanted an agreement whereby they were given fourteen days notice of any industrial action the workforce might contemplate in the future. In negotiations ISTC were able to make some progress on wages but were unable to increase them to the level paid to cleaners (two years earlier) when they were BSC employees because BSC would not make enough money available to cover 'Contract Cleaners'' increased costs. Holidays were increased but the process was to be staggered and the full holiday entitlement that BSC workers had enjoyed when they did the work would not be reached for a number of years. Finally, ISTC had to agree to a lump sum payment to members by 'Contract Cleaners' to 'buy out' the current negotiating date, that is 'Contract Cleaners' were able to move the annual negotiation to a date which suited them.

Finally, if the trade unions could do little to improve the contractors' wages and conditions, surely they could do something about their habit of 'employing' workers off-the-books? An ISTC officer claimed that some ISTC officials at Port Talbot had *refused* to do anything about a particular contractor who was using off-the-books labour, and *in general* the craft unions were supposed to have had more success in this field, as in other aspects of work with contractors. Both sections of the AUEW (Construction and Engineering) claimed that they had gone through the Port Talbot works with a fine tooth comb and that they had checked all the contractors' books. Furthermore, they wrote to the contractors twice a year warning them of 'malpractices', but how effective were these warnings? An AUEW branch official explained that he might tell his full-time officer to investigate a case where a contractor was suspected of using off-the-books labour, but the case would then be referred to national headquarters and this would be the last they heard of it. The branch was hamstrung, they

'need the region to do it, but the full-timer never catches anyone.'

He was not, for example, on site at night time when a lot of off-the-books work went on. In fact, both the branch officials and regional officer were handicapped by their union's policy. There was no incentive for a member to tell the union of employers' 'malpractices' because the union then gave him or her Hobson's Choice: either they shopped him or her to the DHSS or s/he paid the moneys s/he had falsely claimed in benefits into union funds. The union might be well advised to consider the advantages of an amnesty for members who have worked off-the-books[6].

**Footnotes**

1. Certainly the task of convincing BSC managers that they had made a mistake was not an easy one. Take for example the experience of ISTC negotiators at BSC Lackenby:

    'Early in 1983, we entered into negotiations on management's proposals to replace direct labour with contractors, in the BOS and Concast areas. According to BSC £42,000 per annum would be saved, should their proposals be implemented. In our initial meeting, the apparent cost comparisons placed us in a very difficult position. However, when we closely questioned management on certain aspects, it became clear that many areas of comparison had been deliberately overlooked by BSC.

    'Subsequent to very detailed negotiations, we managed to turn the whole situation round, thereby proving that the cheapest and best method of operation would be to invest some capital £80,000 and retain direct labour. The results of our endeavours in that first meeting seemed to leave the management team in a state of shock: they asked to stand adjourned, to check our figures. Three further meetings were held on the subject, each time management producing revised proposals, only to result on every occasion with us managing to precisely emulate what had transpired in the very first meeting.

'...over a considerable period of time, probably 6-9 months, management quite consciously engineered the existing fork lift trucks into disrepair, thereby causing losses in the region of at least £80-100,000 over that period. Without question, they were prepared to sacrifice that amount of cash, attempting to demonstrate how inefficient direct labour was, compared to the contractors tender. Obviously, we are pleased to report that their strategy has backfired!'

2. The Contractors' Committee was certainly not responsible for the union's success in the cold mill packing dispute. The branch official involved in the dispute thought that the unions' victory had been somewhat fortunate:

'It was just because one or two people managed to get down and work it out.'

3. Similar tactics were used by BSC on other occasions, for example where increased flexibility was demanded of the BSC workforce.

4. The multi-union committee was similarly ineffective where it was asked to resist BSC proposals to reduce employment which were unrelated to the use of contractors.

5. Certainly some trade unions at other BSC plants appear to be better at compromises than the Port Talbot unions. This may be proof of the *particularly* damaging legacy of *Port Talbot's* Slimline (see Chapter Two), although a source close to senior officials at the plant suggested that there were other factors at play. He suggested that some officials had a personal interest in the success of certain contracting firms. Note that the enthusiasm shown by trade union officials at Llanwern, when given the opportunity to criticise colleagues at other BSC plants, is evidence of another major division in steel trade unionism: the division between regions. Llanwern officials were more than happy to criticise Port Talbot and, especially, Ravenscraig, as long as BSC had not made its final decision about which of the five remaining integrated steelworks would be closed.

6. Italian trade unions have also, apparently, shown little interest in taking action to stop the spread of off-the-books work (De Grazia 1984: 87).

Chapter Eight

# A Balance Sheet

*Productivity and the Return to Financial Viability*

Readers may remember from Chapter Two that the Slimline agreement set BSC Port Talbot's 'authorised manning' at 5,701 with the capacity to produce 1.4 million tonnes of steel per annum. Table 2.1 in Chapter Two showed the effect of Slimline and subsequent agreements on 'actual manning' at BSC Port Talbot: by 1984 employment at the steelworks had fallen to 4,808 (from 12,415 at the end of December 1979). In 1984 BSC Port Talbot produced 1.9 million tonnes of crude steel (table 8.1), an increase of a third over Slimline capacity. Indeed, table 8.1 shows that 1984 output was higher than in 1969, 1970, 1975 and 1977. BSC Port Talbot was now producing similar tonnages of steel to its output in the 1970s but with a third of the number of employees. It is clear therefore that productivity — defined as tonnes of steel per employee — increased substantially in the 1980s.

Increased productivity at BSC Port Talbot was due to technological change, changes in the working practices of BSC employees, and the increased use of contractors. The most expensive items of new technology installed at BSC Port Talbot in the 1980s were the Concast plant, which began production in 1982, and the refurbished hot strip mill which was in operation by 1986[1]. In addition to these major installations a number of minor projects were completed between 1981 and 1986. For example, new coke ovens were put into operation in 1981 and new computers for

**Table 8.1 BSC Port Talbot Crude Steel Output (tonnes per annum) 1969-1984**

| 1969 | 1 797 520 | 1977 | 1 653 395 |
|------|-----------|------|-----------|
| 1970 | 1 660 066 | 1978 | 1 929 425 |
| 1971 | 2 144 591 | 1979 | 2 314 528 |
| 1972 | 2 509 473 | 1980 | 902 735* |
| 1973 | 2 798 640 | 1981 | 1 785 156 |
| 1974 | 2 038 209 | 1982 | 1 653 773 |
| 1975 | 1 829 406 | 1983 | 1 818 873 |
| 1976 | 2 097 142 | 1984 | 1 921 204 |

*Three months steel strike

**Source:** BSC Personnel Department

production control were purchased in the following year. In 1982 BSC estimated its investment over four years at BSC Port Talbot at £400 million. This figure of course *excludes* the £170 million spent on refurbishing the hot strip mill.

Even though we already have a separate heading for the effect of contractors on increased productivity, the reader should recognise that contractors were responsible for the installation (and subsequent maintenance) of the new technology. We heard in Chapter Four, for example, that 2,500 contracting workers were at work on the hot strip mill in 1985. Of course if this work had been done before 1980 BSC would still have been required to use outside contractors, but not as many since at that time BSC directly employed workers who were responsible for new installations.

Contractors contributed to increased productivity through the installation of new technology, but contractors also contributed to increased productivity through their effect on the working practices of *BSC* employees. In 1980 the Chief Executive of BSC, Bob Scholey, explained what was required of those BSC employees who remained after the redundancies:

> '... internationally competitive manning standards ... These standards assume the willingness of Trade Union organisations and individual employees to cooperate fully in a philosophy of manning, the organisation of work and the provision of employee services comparable with practices in Europe, but far removed from traditions in the public sector in the UK.'
>
> (House of Commons Committee on Welsh Affairs 1980)

The increased use of contractors — or rather the *threat* of contractors — helped BSC to achieve these aims because BSC workers were forced to match the contractors in order to hold onto their jobs. For example, using some contracting workers in repair and maintenance solved the 'industrial relations' difficulties BSC had faced from craft workers even where the work was still done by BSC employees. If they threatened resistance over working practices BSC could simply counter with the threat of contractors. Of course it was not simply the craft workers that were affected in this way: BSC were able to force all sorts of workers to accept changes in working practices (and therefore in employment levels) by proposing to put their jobs out to contract.

We now turn to the *direct* contribution of contracting workers to increased productivity. If the labour of contracting workers had simply been substituted for the labour of BSC employees on an equal basis there would have been no increase in productivity as a direct effect of using contractors. But contracting workers were not substituted on an equal basis.

Firstly, the contractors' working practices were very different from those in force before 1980 when the same work was done by BSC employees. The most extreme examples of changes in working practices were in those cases where BSC had experienced persistent 'industrial relations' difficulties before the work was put out to contractors, for instance in the case of the bricklayers who re-lined furnaces. To put it bluntly, bringing in contractors to do the work meant that BSC bricklayers would not threaten management with strike action, but this is too limiting an interpretation of 'industrial relations' difficulties. Thus BSC had had to pay dearly, through wage increases, if they wanted these workers to accept employment reductions or changes in working practices. Furthermore, as an ex-BSC worker explained, the strength of some groups of workers forced BSC to 'carry' workers who were 'incompetent'[2]. All of this applies most directly to the craft workers employed by BSC — the electricians, engineers and bricklayers. All of these groups had been involved in protracted strikes, all were renowned for causing difficulties over job demarcation and wage differentials between craft and production workers, and most lost their jobs to contractors in 1980[3].

Secondly, the increased use of contractors led to improved productivity because the contracting workers were not — in contrast to the BSC workers they replaced — at work full time and/or throughout the year. At this point the reader should remember that a steelworks is not an assembly line:

> 'A BSC Port Talbot steelworker, who had worked at the plant for 28 years, was dismissed after he was found two miles from his workplace without permission ... [It was alleged]
>
> '"He was apprehended by a works security guard outside the works perimeter and some 2 miles away from his place of work. The report that management received was that he was on his bicycle. He has since acknowledged he was going to attend to his fishing lines."
>
> '"... as far as he was concerned it had been common practice over the years to leave the plant and attend to fishing lines as soon as their work was finished"'.

(*South Wales Evening Post*, 11 November 1983)

The phrase "as soon as their work was finished" suggests that for some employees at BSC there was, and is, not enough work to keep them occupied all the time. This is both true and quite sensible: unoccupied time is in the nature of certain jobs — for example, the work of a technician who deals with breakdowns — and it need not imply that 'too many' workers are employed. As BSC managers *used* to say, 'craftsmen in steel are a necessary evil': they wanted the plant to run smoothly but if it was running smoothly then the craft workers weren't working. The solution to this problem was, of course, to use contracting workers who could be called onto the site only when they were needed.

Soon after the mass redundancies of 1980 had taken effect BSC announced that there had been substantial improvements in productivity, especially at Llanwern and Port Talbot (Morgan 1983: 184-185). Unfortunately, it is impossible to quantify the effect of contractors on BSC Port Talbot's productivity. In the first place, it is impossible to calculate the total productivity increase from 1980, for two reasons. Firstly, the *quality* of the product has improved and so comparisons before and after 1980 would not compare like with like. Secondly, even if the problem of quality is put to one side, we cannot calculate the overall improvement in productivity because we do not know how to take account of the contracting workers. In fact BSC chooses to forget all about contracting workers when making productivity calculations (which are usually expressed as 'man hours per tonne'). According to a source close to the Chief Executive, BSC do not, and will not, make allowances for contractors in their productivity figures. BSC's figures therefore give an inaccurate impression of improvements in productivity[4].

If we do a rough-and-ready calculation on the basis of tables 2.1 and 8.1, productivity at BSC Port Talbot worked out at 186 tonnes of steel per employee (including staff) in 1979 and 400 tonnes per employee in 1984. This calculation gives a rate of increase in productivity very close to that quoted by BSC senior management (see, for example, *Port Talbot Guardian*, 10 November 1983), but if the maximum estimate of the number of contracting workers (excluding those at work on new projects) is added to the official count of BSC employees, productivity in 1984 drops to 282 tonnes per person. This would give a productivity increase of fifty per cent between 1979 and 1982, but this figure assumes that BSC used no contracting workers *at all* in 1979. If these workers were added to the calculation the level of productivity increase would be reduced, however this would still be a misleading figure because the calculation assumes that 2,000 contracting workers were at work full-time and all-year-round in 1984. We know this was not the case and so a proper calculation would reduce the 2,000 to a lower (full-time equivalent) figure which would push up the rate of productivity in 1984. These adjustments would probably result in a productivity increase *in excess* of fifty per cent between 1980 and 1984. However, what proportion of this very approximate figure resulted from the increased use of contractors is anybody's guess.

Even if it were possible to calculate the indirect contribution of contractors to improved productivity, we would have no figure to put on the contractors' direct contribution because BSC will not, or cannot[5], provide a figure for the total labour hours for contracting workers. Let us say, instead, that the increased use of contractors had a 'substantial' effect on productivity.

If it is impossible to quantify the effect of contractors on output per worker, it is equally impossible to calculate the effect of contractors on the *cost* of producing each tonne of steel. In fact improved productivity in the sense of improved output per worker does not necessarily lead to reduced cost per tonne. A simple example will prove this point: imagine that a firm reduces employment for the same volume of output but increases wages so that the total wage bill increases even though fewer workers are employed. In this case productivity increases but so does the cost of each unit of output. This did not, of course, happen at BSC Port Talbot. However, there were other factors which might lead to increased costs even while productivity increased.

Firstly, there were some occasions when BSC put work out to contract which might have been done more cheaply by BSC employees (working overtime for example)[6]. Thus even though the contracting workers' productivity was higher than that of BSC workers, BSC was simply paying the contracting firm too much for the job. One of the ex-BSC workers interviewed by Griselda Leaver explained that

> 'This business of contractors ...it's going to bump their costs up in the end ... Well, before I worked for Leeris I had been involved in dealing with the contracted labour at BSC. Now, we paid Leeris 3.78 per hour for a labourer, so when I went to work for Leeris myself I thought forty hours times the best part of 3.78 ... less stamps and that ... it would be a good deal ... But when I got it I was only on 1.40 an hour ... the rest had gone to the contractor ... so I went along and asked him "What's going on here ... 1.40 an hour ...?" and he said "What's wrong with that?" ... so I said "We paid you 3.78 when I was in the Abbey" ... so he said "I'll give you extra as long as you don't tell the rest of the men" ... I got the extra ... He was charging BSC 3.78 and paying 1.40 ... and I'd have to pay my stamp from that.'[7]

In large part miscalculations of the relative costs of direct labour and contractors can be explained by the atmosphere of panic which accompanied all the decisions made by BSC managers in 1980 (and for some time after 1980). From what we know (see Chapter Two) of the way in which the Slimline plan was worked out at Port Talbot, it is clear that local management had insufficient time for any reliable costing exercises which might allow them to evaluate alternative means of reducing employment in excess of the reduction in output. When compared to the procedures laid down by Harrigan (1985) — an advocate of contracting-out — BSC's 'planning' seems woefully inadequate. For example, managers had little time to request quotes from likely contractors which might allow them to consider the relative merits of direct labour versus contractors before they put their plan before the BSC board. Indeed, it is highly unlikely that local managers knew even *how many* contractors' workers they would need in any part of the works (or in total). There were departments — cleaning and internal transport being the most obvious — where it must have been known from the start of the exercise that contractors would take over all of the work. But in other cases managers can have had little clear idea of the mix of direct labour and contractors which would be required, especially since they could not anticipate the full effect of flexible working on the productivity of those BSC employees who remained after the redundancies. (By spring 1981, BSC managers had some breathing space and made minor alterations to their plans, for example they decided not to contract-out catering).

Secondly, there were cases where using contractors had *hidden* costs[8]. The BSC workers I talked to during my fieldwork were keen to persuade me to investigate the possibility that contracting was not necessarily cost-effective. In fact some of them had been trying to persuade their union leaders of this for a considerable time. Take, for instance, the complaint made in 1981 by a local official (at another steelworks) of the National Union of Blastfurnacemen (NUB):

> 'The BSC obviously claim that the economics of the exercise are for the good of the industry, but personally I think it is total madness and that the Steel Committee should be making an in-depth study into this subject.'

BSC workers made frequent complaints about the poor standards of the contractors' work. They believed this difference in standards should be taken into account when assessing the cost advantages of contractors. Similar complaints of poor standards were made by *contracting firms* which had undertaken work at the steelworks for many years.These old-established contractors said that the standard of work on engineering and construction contracts had fallen since 1980. Since some of these firms had subsequently been supplanted[9], there was obviously a large element of self-interest in their complaints. The same could be said of the complaints made by BSC employees that the maintenance work done by contractors was shoddy compared to the standards in force before 1980 when much of the work was done by BSC workers. They even claimed that this had affected production. Of course, there are many other reasons for production breakdowns and it is impossible to establish to what extent contractors were to blame.

In fact, support for the BSC workers' contention that contractors did not, on occasion, do the work properly, came from the contracting workers themselves. Several of the contracting workers I talked to knew of occasions when BSC workers had been brought in after a contract was completed in order to rectify the mistakes made by the contractor. This was later confirmed by trade union sources. Indeed, union officials at Llanwern explained that this was one of the reasons they liked to keep BSC workers and contracting workers geographically apart, so that they were not working in the same part of the plant:

> 'We need the contractors to be responsible for themselves. We don't want to be blamed if the contractors cock it up. It's an insurance.'

BSC would deny that they have been so foolish as to actively pursue a policy which led, for instance, to production breakdowns. Nevertheless, BSC may have taken a short-sighted view on contracting because they were subject to short-term pressures. They had to cut costs this week and not the next, so management preferred, for example, to have buildings painted only occasionally or not at all since the cost of the damage thereby incurred could be ignored since it would fall in a future financial year. In any event, it is in the very nature of such costs that they should remain hidden, at least for some time[10]. Meanwhile BSC has returned to 'financial viability' (see Chapter One) and we can *infer* that costs per tonne of steel have fallen. The increased use of contractors has contributed to this process because it had reduced labour costs.

Firstly, contracting workers did not replace BSC employees on an equal basis: there were fewer of them and so the total labour costs of the work they did were reduced. Secondly, contracting workers were not at work on a full-time basis or throughout the year. They were paid only for their time at work and this also depressed labour costs. Indeed labour costs fell even in those few cases where contracting workers received *higher* wages than BSC employees since high wages were only paid for a short time. (Thus in Chapter Five we saw that *skilled* contracting workers often had the shortest spells at work).

Thirdly, hourly wage rates paid to contracting workers were frequently lower than those which had been paid to BSC employees for the same work. This had an especially dramatic effect on labour costs in those cases (described earlier in this chapter) where BSC had found its own employees particularly troublesome[11]. Fourthly, and particularly importantly, the increased use of contractors depressed labour costs because the contracting workers received little or no fringe benefits, for example *pensions*[12].

Finally, the reduction in *direct* labour costs was augmented by a reduction in overheads. For example, the overhead costs of using BSC employees instead of contractors included the cost of compliance with the Health and Safety at Work Act. If contractors did not comply with the Act then BSC had the work done more cheaply. BSC Port Talbot was a more dirty and dangerous place to work in as a result of the increased use of contractors (the same may also apply to other industries where the use of contractors has recently been increased, *Guardian*, 21 January 1987).

A summary of the conclusions reached in this section may be useful to the reader. Firstly, BSC's productivity — defined as tonnes of steel per worker — increased. This increase in productivity was due to three changes in the way steel was produced: new technology was installed, the working practices of BSC employees were altered, and contractors were brought in. The increased use of contractors contributed *indirectly* to the improvement in productivity through new technology and changes in BSC employees' working practices; but contractors also contributed to increased productivity *directly*. Contractors used different working practices from those used by BSC before work was put out to contract and contracting workers were not employed full-time and/or throughout the year. Unfortunately the effect of the increased use of contractors on productivity cannot be quantified (indeed we are not even able to put an accurate figure on the overall level of productivity increase let alone to isolate the contribution made by contractors). Increased productivity need not mean that unit costs were reduced and in some respects the increased use of contractors may have carried extra costs, including hidden ones. However, BSC has returned to profit and we must assume that costs per tonne have fallen. The increased use of contractors has contributed to lower unit costs because it has led to lower (direct *and* indirect) labour costs.

### Productivity and the Return to Mass Unemployment
In 1980 BSC presented their Slimline plan as an unfortunate necessity which had been forced on them by falling demand for steel. The name Slimline implies the need to trim production to realistic levels. However, the document which detailed the Slimline plan was called *Return to Financial Viability* and this title implies a rather different aim[13]. It is clear from the documentary evidence of the time that the reductions in employment at BSC were produced by more stringent government financial controls and not by over-production of steel. This seems to have been the opinion of the House of Commons Committee on Welsh Affairs (1980) and it was certainly the opinion of ISTC:

> 'BSC's proposal to cut production to 15 m.t.p.a. and employment by almost 50,000 are not based upon an economic appraisal of the world and domestic steel markets. The analysis of the *Business Proposal*

*[Return to Financial Viability]* by independent accountants ... clearly traces its origins to a callous and uncompromising decision by the Secretary of State for Industry to allow only £450 million under cash limits during the current year. This is the real *driving force behind these decisions and BSC stands guilty of hiding it and presenting its solution as an unavoidable economic necessity.*' (ISTC, 1980: 84, see also Upham, 1980)

ISTC's opinion was confirmed in subsequent years by events at Port Talbot and elsewhere. Thus a Slimline Port Talbot was intended to produce less steel but by 1984 Port Talbot was producing thirty-six per cent more steel than Slimline capacity dictated, and with 1,000 less employees than Slimline 'authorised manning'. Slimline had been presented as an unavoidable consequence of reduced demand but turned out to be a way of producing increased output with less employees in the belief that this would return BSC to financial viability.

We saw in Chapter Two that the Conservative Government which was elected in 1979 told BSC that operating losses would no longer be funded and that less public money would be made available for BSC in future. According to Kevin Morgan,

'The Government's initial refusal to extend BSC's operations external financing limit, together with its imposition of an impossible breakeven target for 1980/1, represented the most stringent cash limits ever imposed on a nationalised industry in Britain.'

(Morgan, 1983: 181-2)

Although BSC did not break even as quickly as the Government wished, 'financial viability' was eventually achieved in 1985/6 (see Chapter One). Does this mean that the Government's 'cash limits' were successful?[14]

We have already seen in this chapter that some aspects of Slimline may have had hidden costs *for BSC*, but the cash limits strategy which produced Slimline also produced hidden *public* costs. For example, at the end of the first section of this chapter I cited four ways in which the increased use of contractors contributed to the return to financial viability through lower labour costs. In each case lower labour costs for BSC led to increased public costs.

Firstly, since contracting workers did not replace BSC employees on a worker-for-worker basis, the state had to bear the cost of welfare benefits to some redundants who remained out of work. Secondly, the state had to provide welfare payments to contracting workers during *their* frequent spells of unemployment (and sometimes even when they were in work). Thirdly, low hourly wages for contracting workers were made up by ECSC cash (see Chapter Four). Finally the state took over responsibility for pensions (together with some other indirect labour costs) for that part of BSC's labour force which was provided by contractors.

ECSC cash was provided by the EEC rather than the British Government, however it was still *public* money (some of which was provided by British tax-payers). The fact that the EEC should provide make-up pay raises some interesting questions all the same. ECSC money was originally intended to ease the social consequences of a reduction in steel output and *not* to help BSC to attempt to compete more effectively with the steel industries of Britain's European partners, *including* those in other member countries of the EEC which helped to pay for the restructuring. This make-up pay was supposed to help their supernumerary steelworkers to find jobs outside steel *but in fact represented a hidden subsidy to BSC*[15]. Firstly, it eased the workforce's acceptance of employment reductions and, particularly, of the increased use of contractors. It therefore helped BSC to restructure employment as they wished. Secondly, make-up allowed contractors to pay lower wages when they employed redundant steelworkers and this meant BSC's labour costs were being directly subsidised with EEC money. What did the EEC get in return? Apparently nothing, since BSC Port Talbot's output was soon back to pre-Slimline levels. Finally, EEC cash allowed BSC to do one other thing that we must assume was not intended when the money was given out. It allowed them to privatise parts of UK steel production. If EEC money was paid out in order to allow BSC to reduce output and yet they used it to privatise production (and to attempt to become more competitive), might not the EEC be justified in demanding a refund?

In any event BSC's achievement of financial viability in the wake of cash limits appears to have been dependent on hidden public subsidies to steelmaking (including EEC subsidies). All of these subsidies represent hidden public *costs* since British tax-payers (and the citizens of the EEC) eventually picked up the tab. However, they were associated with public costs which were borne in other ways, for example by the people of Port Talbot, who were now much more likely to experience unemployment. This point is ably summarised by Kevin Morgan:

> 'BSC is now moving into a breakeven position via the classic capitalist displacement mechanism: its financial crisis is being displaced and translated into an acute social crisis for its redundant workers and their host localities.'
>
> (Morgan, 1983: 194)

The Government's role in creating the 'crisis' in the steeltowns is complicated. Firstly, the use of cash limits signalled an end to the policy (pursued by successive governments) whereby steel was used to help areas which could not of themselves generate sufficient employment, especially South Wales (Morgan, 1983: 194). Chapters Two and Three showed that Port Talbot was particularly vulnerable to any alteration in government policy. This was because the town had continued to grow and thrive only through the intervention of successive governments which sought to create employment there. They did not do this for Port Talbot's sake, but for the sake of workers in the surrounding region (including the mining valleys) who were no longer required by private industry.

Port Talbot was a convenient site for the new jobs which governments felt it necessary to create. Thus in Chapter Three we learnt that employment in Port Talbot in particular, and Wales in general, was largely created by government intervention. Governments put steelworks where work was needed. This was why the steelworks were built in Port Talbot and why the works received Government support at crucial stages in its development. If profits alone were what mattered the town of Port Talbot would not have continued to grow in the second half of the twentieth century. The Talbot family no longer had a use for it and neither did the Great Western Railway, but successive governments decided to give Port Talbot steel to make it viable[16] — a mixed blessing some might say — although this policy never altered the basic facts. Port Talbot was only safe so long as the government *kept believing* in using the steel industry as a form of regional aid. When one Government stopped believing in this the effects on employment in Port Talbot were sudden and dramatic, however according to the Government, this decline in employment should only be temporary.

The Conservative Government which was elected in 1979 (and its successor, also Conservative) appeared to believe that the previous (regional) policy was not simply mistaken but the *reverse* of the correct policy. Other governments had used regional aid to make up for a shortfall in employment but this Government thought that the shortfall in employment was *caused* by regional aid and the rest of the apparatus of state intervention. Instead of creating 'artificial' jobs, governments should be reducing state intervention and so improving profitability. This would create the right climate for the growth of 'real', that is *more productive*[17], employment.

In these terms Port Talbot was certainly blessed with more 'real' jobs after 1980 — the increase in productivity and profitability at BSC attest to this fact — but Port Talbot has also been blessed with mass unemployment. The Government which created productive employment in Port Talbot could certainly explain why unemployment should increase at the same time: when we resolve to substitute 'real' jobs for 'artificial' ones we have to acknowledge the fact that 'artificial' jobs are concentrated in certain areas. This means that, for a time, such areas will experience higher than average unemployment (c.f. Morgan, 1983: 1984): turning 'artificial' jobs into 'real' ones creates unemployment since 'real' jobs are more productive. In Port Talbot this does not mean simply that those who *don't* have 'real' jobs are unemployed since many of those who do have 'real' jobs are unemployed for much of the year (because they are more productive these jobs don't provide work all year round). In either case, however, the removal of 'artificial' jobs will supposedly create the right conditions for a return to full employment in the longer term.

The description of employment trends in Chapter Three gives no grounds for believing that there has been real growth in employment (of any kind) in Port Talbot, but perhaps insufficient time has elapsed for us to make a fair assessment of the success of the new policy? In large part the structure of British industry was created by the post-war process of nationalisation and state intervention in private industry and the slate cannot be wiped clean immediately. Nevertheless, it is difficult to see how the creation of 'real' jobs will ever create the right conditions for growth in employment, not least because this policy actually seems to create the right conditions for further *decline* in employment in places like Port Talbot. This brings us to the final aspect of the Government's role in the steeltowns' crisis.

The Government's 'real' jobs policy has, in some areas at least, created the conditions for 'jobless growth', that is where growth in demand for goods or services produces increased output but little or no increase in employment. For example, it would take very little extra recruitment to produce a great deal more steel at BSC Port Talbot. In 1985, according to BSC management, *current* employment levels could be stretched to produce 2 million tonnes per annum instead of the normal 1.7, and an increase of only nine per cent in the number of employees was required in order to produce 2.3 million tonnes. (By late 1988, output actually exceeded the latter figure and was planned to rise to 4 million tonnes.)

That jobless growth is now possible owes something to the expenditure of government funds since public spending paid for the technological advances described at the beginning of this chapter. It was noted in Chapter Three that the *form* of aid to Port Talbot has changed. One of the differences was that the new type of aid actually led to further job losses in steel but we can now add that it also contributed to future jobless growth.

To summarise, the second half of this chapter has shown, firstly, that the changes made by BSC in 1980 were a response to cash limits imposed by the Conservative Government. Secondly, this cash limits strategy was found to have hidden public costs (including costs to the EEC). Thirdly, this strategy contributed to rising unemployment by withdrawing (regional) aid which was necessary if places like Port Talbot were to have anything like full employment, by *directly* reducing employment and by ensuring that future growth in output would not produce commensurate gains in employment. One further conclusion follows from the third part of this summary. If, in some areas at least, substituting 'real' jobs for 'artificial' ones creates unemployment, then we are no longer faced with a choice between 'artificial' jobs and 'real' jobs but between 'artificial' jobs and unemployment. If the people of Port Talbot are to have full employment once more it will have to be artificially created. But this will not be as easy a task as it once was because the change in government policy has changed the *form* of local industry and so made the employment shortfall worse than ever[18].

**Footnotes**

1. Refurbishment of the hot strip mill consisted largely of the building of new 'stands' including one which reduced the thickness of the steel *several* times by reversing it. The forward end of the hot strip mill was therefore scrapped; the main part of the finishing mill remained unaltered.

2. Or perhaps 'intransigent' would be a better word. There was, as the steelworkers put it, a bit of 'crossing the lines', that is getting out of the plant over the railway lines (avoiding security checks) to go to the pub during a shift. Of course, as Hywel, a technician at BSC says, it still goes on, although less than it did. He finds it happens most frequently on the night shift. There is a lot of 'downtime' on a particular line at the 'arse end' of the process. The lines are 'stopped' (sabotaged) so that people can get off early. Hywel finds the trouble comes an hour before the end of the shift so that he will be unable to fix the breakdown in time for the line to start up again before the end of the shift. By the time he gets there only one man is left — the rest are, he presumes, in the pub.

3. BSC were reluctant to *admit* that they were bringing in contractors in order to change working practices and this reluctance sometimes caused embarrassment in their negotiations with the trade unions. At Lackenby, BSC wanted to contract out fork lift truck operations where it appeared to be obvious that it was cheaper to keep the work in house (see Chapter Seven). BSC's real interest was in work 'discipline' however they could not admit this: as the unions said at the time, 'no doubt this point is avoided for political reasons'. BSC therefore had to argue the case for bringing in contractors on the basis of relative costs while trying to avoid discussing any details of costs with the unions.

4. But note that BSC's increased use of contractors has at least made these productivity figures comparable to those quoted by overseas producers.

5. For instance, how could BSC calculate 'man hours' for contracting workers who were off-the-books? Note that we are also unable to put a figure on the *cost* of contracts since such payments are not listed separately in BSC's accounts. Readers should bear this point in mind during the discussion on unit costs which follows.

5. See Fevre 1986 for further details.

6. See Fevre 1986 for futher details.

7. Details altered to preserve confidentiality: 'Leeris' is a fictitious name for a real firm.

8. See Fevre 1986 for further details. For example, it is not certain that the increased use of contractors reduced BSC's capital costs (c.f. the quote from

Harrigan in Chapter Nine). Many of the contractors on the BSC site used BSC tools and machinery together with other BSC facilities (for which they might or might not be charged) and it was commonly believed that contractors had bought BSC plant and equipment, including transport, at knock-down prices.

9.  See Fevre 1986 for futher details.

10. Although note that other writers have made mention of such costs. Bresnen *et al* (1983) report that construction subcontractors are accused of poor quality work (also see Scase and Goffee, 1982: 143), and Williams *et al* argue that British industry as a whole suffers from similar problems. (Their basic idea is that management makes decisions on the basis of false information about which steps can be taken to improve profits, for example cutting back on preventive maintenance). Readers should also note that the foregoing discussion of hidden costs does not exhaust the list of longer-term costs which may arise from the increased use of contractors. For example, recession in the contractors' industries — concerned with construction and engineering — made them eager to take on new areas of work, including contracts at BSC. Some trade union sources argued that BSC knew from past experience that while they had difficulty in finding contractors in a boom period for these industries, things were much easier in a recession. The extent to which BSC had made use of contractors had varied in the past with the state of demand for the contractors' services from other customers. Thus BSC had *taken back* work from contractors at Llanwern when demand for the contractors' services elsewhere picked up in the early 1970s. One union source predicted:

    'BSC have relied on the recession, the collapse of the construction industry, but it could have cut its own throat.'

11. Note that the increased use of contractors also had an indirect effect on wage costs where the threat of contractors served to limit the pressure for wage increases from *BSC employees*.

12. This pattern has been repeated amongst the contracting workers of other nationalised industries and services. Contracting workers in the NHS, for example, are believed to have few fringe benefits together with low pay and no job security (*Guardian*, 18 April 1986; 21 February 1987).

13. Later agreements to reduce employment at BSC Port Talbot were given *slightly* less misleading titles: *Survival* I and *Survival* II.

14. Cash limits were, in any case, something of a compromise. The Government wanted to sell off BSC but found they could not do so and chose to reduce the cash they provided for BSC instead. This does not, however, mean that the Government ran BSC like a private business. Limits on spending in the private sector are imposed by companies' abilities to raise cash through retaining profits, raising money from shareholders, or borrowing money from banks and others. Private industry does not run its businesses on the basis of arbitrarily imposed cash limits on spending, (although *small* private businesses — especially those which fail — may be similar to nationalised industries in that arbitrary cash limits are imposed on them by the banks which provide the bulk of their funds). In contrast, the cash limits imposed by the Government were completely arbitrary as far as BSC was concerned. They made sense only in relation to Cabinet discussions of spending priorities in the light of the overall levels of public spending and borrowing targeted by the Government.

15. And to the British Government: firstly, it was *intended* to subsidise the costs to the Government of the redundancies and subsequent unemployment. But secondly — and this was presumably *not* intended by the EEC — it allowed the Government to reduce its cash limits for BSC to the extent that ECSC cash aid improved BSC's competitive standing.

16. In this process, it became clear that using steel as regional policy was not necessarily compatible with efficient production. It has often been said — by

people who should know — that the Port Talbot steelworks would have been a more efficient unit if tinplate production had also been sited there. Instead, the tinplate works were established further west, near Llanelli and Swansea, in order to compensate for job losses in those parts of the region.

17. As long as 'artificial' jobs are not defined simply as 'jobs created by the state' then the dividing line between 'real' and 'artificial' jobs becomes less clear than we might imagine. This is because the only alternative definition involves some assessment of *productivity*, for example you can recognise a 'real' job because it replaces two other jobs. One of the original jobs is, by definition, 'artificial'; but *how much* improvement in productivity is necessary to make a job real? One hundred per cent may suffice, but what if our one 'real' job *could have* replaced four other jobs rather than two? Is it then not 'real' but still 'artificial'?

18. Thus Chapter Three gave the impression that, even if the same amount of regional aid was provided as before, Port Talbot would still have a shortfall of jobs. This may also be due, in part, to the greater difficulties of using help to private industry to create employment as opposed to direct job creation using the steel industry (or the construction industry).

# Chapter Nine

# Making Unemployment Work

*'New' Employment Practices*

In the United States, according to Philip Mattera, the idea of a career based on full-time, permanent employment is fast becoming outmoded (1985: 25). Richard Brown, in a *general* article on the future of work in Britain, finds it necessary to discuss the growth of alternatives to permanent employment (1983: 270). Mark Spilsbury, Malcolm Maguire and David Ashton feel that in Britain we may be witnessing 'the disintegration of a long-standing, traditional relationship between employers and employees' (*Guardian*, 24 September 1986). This sort of argument requires some modification, however. In the first place, full-time permanent employment is rather less 'traditional' for women than for men. In the second, the 'tradition' is not an old one: permanent employment contracts only became the norm in the latter half of the twentieth century and 'new' employment practices may represent a *return* to earlier traditions (Meager, 1986; also see the quotations from Beveridge in Chapter Five). Finally, new evidence suggests that alternatives to permanent employment have received more attention than they deserve. According to Pollert (1988), many of the writers quoted here and below have wittingly or unwittingly exaggerated such trends. She concludes that perhaps the only significant evidence for such changes is to be found in public-sector (and privatising) employers like BSC, and in the use of contractors.

The most well-researched area is the *growth in the numbers of temporary workers*. There is some disagreement about the details — for example the size of the companies most likely to use temporary workers — but the (official) Labour Force Survey and surveys by the Institute of Manpower Studies and by Manpower, a temporary employment agency, are agreed on two points. Firstly, the number of temporary workers *has* increased. Secondly, temporary workers are no longer confined to the industries, like construction, which have traditionally used them. For example, both transport and engineering show above average rates of growth for temporary workers. None of the published research mentions *steel* in this context but this may be because reports from *contractors* in any industry are unreliable[1]. They are apparently so accustomed to peculiar employment practices that they find it difficult to distinguish temporary from permanent employees (Meager, 1986: 8).

Something like seven per cent of the working population of Britain in the mid-1980s were temporary workers, and fully two-thirds of companies used some temporaries. In contrast to BSC, most of these firms employed their temporary workers *directly*: eighty per cent of temporaries in the Institute of Manpower Studies survey were directly employed by the user organisation[2]. The proportion of directly employed temporaries increased on the lower rungs of the occupational ladder; however, most temporaries in the lower reaches of the occupational hierarchy were not employed on fixed-term contracts. Meager (1986: 10) describes the usual arrangement as being an '"open-ended" or casual relationship', and this *does* recall the practices of BSC contractors. It also suggests that the growth in temporary work may have been accompanied by an *increase in the numbers of casual workers*.

There is some evidence that sections of the workforce have been returned to the casual status they escaped after the war, a status which Beveridge (amongst others) sought to abolish (see Chapter Five). The TUC found an 'increasingly casual group shut out from regular work' (*Guardian*, 18 February 1985) and this claim is supported by independent research (for example, Ferman *et al*, 1978; De Grazia, 1984; Mattera, 1985). Much research refers to the return of 'casualism' in the construction industry. For example, Bresnen *et al* (1985) quoted the rising proportion of the total construction workforce taken up by employers and the self-employed as evidence of an increasing degree of casualism (also see Moore, 1981). The self-employed, together with many of those classified as employers, found work on a casual basis as sub-contractors (including labour-only subcontract, the 'lump') and so did firms in other industries, especially in engineering and the service industries. Thus, while a few industries[3] still accounted for the majority of self-employed workers, the self-employed made up an increasing proportion of the workforce. Spilsbury, Maguire and Ashton ask whether this reflects

'a preference by employers for hiring such workers on specific task-related contracts, rather than retaining permanent members of the workforce to carry out this work?' (*Guardian*, 24 September 1986)

Bresnen *et al* take pains to point out that the 'lump' in construction should not automatically be thought of as work *off-the-books* (1985; 111) but there is plenty of evidence from other sources which suggests that increasing casualism has been associated with the growth of off-the-books employment. Firms use off-the-books workers in a variety of industries, but especially those where contractors and sub-contractors are numerous (Ferman *et al*, 1978; De Grazia, 1983). Despite the general difficulties of estimating the extent of off-the-books employment (Ferman *et al*, 1978), most commentators conclude that it has increased,both in Britain and elsewhere (Mattera, 1985).

Why has there been an increase in the use of temporary workers, casual workers and off-the-books labour? Not so long ago employers used alternatives to permanent employment, especially temporary work, because they had difficulty in finding permanent employees. Temporary employment was associated with *growth* in employment, particularly in the service sector — for example in office work, in banking, insurance and finance, and in education — but also in oil exploration and exploitation. In places like London and Aberdeen, therefore, temporary work grew out of a shortage of labour and in these circumstances working as a temporary could be quite attractive. In the 1980s, however, there is far less evidence of labour shortage, so has the growth of temporary, casual and off-the-books work occurred because employers have found *new* reasons for using alternatives to permanent employees?

Five reasons for the growth of alternative employment are advanced in the literature. The first is *lower indirect labour costs*. Manpower found that reduction in indirect costs was one of the reasons advanced by employers for the use of both temporary workers and subcontractors (*Sunday Times*, 16 February 1986). Nigel Meager reached similar results but added that such 'new rationales' for employing temporaries were not mentioned by all employers and were most common amongst those (manufacturing) firms which were using temporaries for the first time. When listing fringe benefits saved by using temporary workers, employers were especially likely to mention pensions (Meager, 1986). The literature on casual work and work off-the-books confirms that lower indirect labour costs have played a part in the growth of alternatives to permanent employment, and also mentions an area of indirect cost saving which is often neglected: the costs of safeguarding health and safety at work (Mattera, 1985).

Since the health and safety costs are so often neglected in the research literature, it is worth adding a little detail here. In the previous chapter it was suggested that BSC Port Talbot had become a more dirty and dangerous place to work in following the increased use of outside contractors. In 1983 the Factory Inspectorate concluded that this was a *general* trend:

'The number of people killed in accidents in industry has risen for the first time in several years, Mr James Hammer, Chief Inspector of Factories, said yesterday.

'He blamed the rise in fatal accidents from 236 in 1981 to 256 in 1982 partly on an increase in maintenance work by outside contractors. Too often, outside contractors, unfamiliar with the equipment they were

servicing, worked without proper control or supervision, he said ...
'The increased use of outside contractors was accompanied by reduced manning levels in many companies, Mr Hammer said ...
'In one steelworks ... a survey of 11 haulage contractors' vehicles found that nine were unfit for use on the highway but were kept for use in the works. The defects were due to neglect rather than to particular conditions on site, the report said.'

*(Times*, 14 December 1983).

The second common explanation for the use of alternative employment practices was *increased flexibility*. The Institute of Manpower Studies research, reported by Meager, analysed employers' reasons for using temporary workers in some detail. Amongst the reasons were:

'— the need to consolidate and extend productivity gains made during the recession
— greater volatility and uncertainty in product markets
— a faster rate of technological change.'

(Meager 1986: 7)

As a result, employers felt they needed 'more workforce flexibility'. This need was also reported by employers in the survey by Manpower (*Sunday Times*, 16 February 1986), and was cited as one of the reasons for the growth in casual work and work off-the-books. According to John Atkinson (1984) all of these alternatives to permanent employment amount to a general movement towards the creation of the 'flexible firm'. In the flexible firm traditional employment practices are changed so that 'radically different approaches to employment can be pursued for different types of worker' (*Guardian*, 18 April 1984). Atkinson's theory has received support from the United States: in a recently-published management manual, Harrigan explains that there is — or should be — 'a new, flexible approach to organization', and adds that

'It is hard to imagine a better way for a company to grow than by having people work for it as if they were part of the company without having expensive capital investments committed to the work they do. More managers should consider contracting-out many tasks performed in-house right now. (1985: 4).

Harrigan lists steel as one of the prime examples of an industry which would benefit from adopting this recommendation (1985: 64)

*Lower direct labour costs* are the third reason why employers might use alternative employment practices. The TUC thought that both temporary and casual workers were over-represented in low-paid jobs (*Guardian*, 18 February 1985). However, although low wages were frequently mentioned in relation to casual and off-the-books work, there was little evidence of employers increasing their use of *temporary workers* because this reduced direct labour costs. For example, neither the survey by the Institute of Manpower Studies nor the survey by the temporary employment agency Manpower suggested that reduced direct labour costs were behind the growth of temporary work. There may be some confusion here, however. Employers responding to these surveys may simply have compared the *hourly* labour costs of temporary workers with the *hourly* rates paid to permanent workers: a comparison of *annual* direct labour costs might have revealed that reductions in total wages were achieved by using temporary workers. Thus while Nigel Meager did not (on the basis of the Institute of Manpower Studies survey) give much weight to lower direct labour costs amongst his 'new rationales' for employing temporaries, he added this question:

> 'In an economic sense, does the growth of temporary work represent a mis-allocation of resources, a divergence between private and social cost? It might, for example, be argued that in expanding the use of temporary workers, employers are shifting to the state (and to households) the costs not only of training, but of income support for these workers during the "troughs" in company workloads. Thus the net social benefits to the economy of an increase in temporary work may be less than the sum of the benefits to individual employers.'
>
> (Meager, 1986: 15).

If temporary workers require income support then their employers are paying out less in wages. Higher hourly labour costs for some (but by no means all) temporaries obscure lower total labour costs for the employers who use them.

The fourth common explanation for the use of alternatives to permanent employment is that employers use these alternatives in order to *change industrial relations* in their firms. Again there is little mention of this effect in the literature on temporary workers but industrial relations receive considerable attention in writing on casual and off-the-books work. In general, employers are thought to use casual or off-the-books workers because, at least in part, they can reduce the percentage of their workforce which belongs to a trade union (see for example Bresnen *et al*, 1985: 118).

The final explanation for the increasing use of alternative employment practices is that employers have been stimulated to introduce such practices by *changing circumstances*. Meager found that employers' use of temporaries was ad hoc and 'rarely part of a well-formulated manning strategy', and Atkinson prefers to talk of a 'pragmatic and opportunistic shift towards these more flexible forms of manning' rather than of a 'new orthodoxy' (*Guardian*, 15 April 1984). To what changes in circumstances are employers responding? In part the argument relies on a reversal of the previous explanation: employers used alternatives to permanent employment because changes in industrial relations allowed them to do so. Thus Meager found that employers mentioned more "benign" industrial relations in connection with the increased use of temporary workers, but Meager's employers also mentioned rising *unemployment* (1986: 15) and this topic deserves more lengthy treatment.

*Unemployment and New Employment Practices*
Most of the existing explanations for the use of new employment practices also apply in the specific case of BSC[4], but these explanations are not complete. It is not so much that there are particular gaps in the research literature, but that there is no convincing attempt to look beyond the reasons given by *employers* for their use of new employment practices to a more general level of explanation. In other words, there is as yet no *theory* of the new employment practices. To conclude this chapter, and this book, I want to use the example of new employment practices at BSC Port Talbot to make a contribution to this theory[5]. Such a theory will not explain why BSC restructured employment in 1980 and subsequent years or the plain and obvious effects of restructuring on the workforce since both of these topics have been discussed at length in earlier chapters. Rather, the theory should attempt to explain the fundamental changes which have been wrought in relations between employers and employees as a result of restructuring (especially) in the public sector (and during privatisation).

The Institute of Manpower Studies survey reported by Nigel Meager was unable to indicate the extent to which temporary workers were recruited from the ranks of the unemployed. However, this did not prevent Meager from suggesting that there is some relationship between the increasing popularity of new employment practices and rising unemployment. According to Meager, rising unemployment is one of the reasons why employers have changed their employment practices. Presumably, this is a variation on a simple argument which can be applied in all cases where employers want to make changes their employees will not welcome: employers can use a carrot (bonus payments for example) or a stick (the threat of the sack) to secure the workers' cooperation. The existence of mass unemployment allows employers to favour the stick rather than the carrot in their dealings with employees, since the workers know that there are now unemployed workers who may replace them if they do not comply.

This simple argument only holds if, as unemployment rises, the workers' *fear* of becoming unemployed increases. Chapters Five and Seven include some examples of the way in which employers can use this fear and Chapter Eight shows how the argument might be extended a stage further. The fear of unemployment leads workers to increase *productivity* but then, assuming 'jobless growth', a circle is established: fear of unemployment increases productivity which increases unemployment which increases fear which raises productivity and so on[6]. There are, however, two difficulties with this theory.

Firstly, there are limits to the effect (on productivity for example) of an *abstract* fear of unemployment. The benefits (to employers) of increased unemployment are limited because the unemployed remain outside the factory gates. Workers in employment may not believe that employers will go to the trouble of training a new workforce in order to replace them. They are, in any case, not as desperate as the unemployed; no matter how much they are disciplined by the fear of redundancy the employer may suspect that the existing workforce are receiving higher wages for less product than the unemployed would offer. To take an extreme example, how useful is mass unemployment in Sunderland to an employer in Swindon? The same principle applies even where the employer operates in an area of high unemployment: the simple fact remains that existing workers are in employment. The cooperation employees will extend to employers to *hold onto* their jobs may be rather less whole-hearted than the cooperation which the unemployed would offer in order to *get* a job.

Secondly, the simple argument no longer fits the facts, or rather some of the facts. The circle of unemployment-fear-increased productivity-unemployment assumes that there is a clear dividing line between the employed and the unemployed. The unemployed are only brought into the circle in the imagination of employees. Unemployment is conceived as something *out there*, a completely separate thing to work which only influences workers indirectly: unemployment is the 'scrap heap' to which those in employment fear they will be condemned. I have tried to argue throughout this book that such a conception is no longer adequate. Popular articles about unemployment in places like Port Talbot where mass redundancies have occurred still make frequent use of the analogy with a scrap heap. There are places with traditional industries and their traditional workers are, sadly, no longer needed. But this is simply not true: in Port Talbot only half of the unemployed were on any sort of scrap heap (that is, were long-term unemployed).

We might be able to account, in part, for this if employers were *recruiting* amongst the unemployed. This would deal with some of the other objections to the simple argument about the relationship between rising unemployment and the new employment practices. If employers recruit the unemployed it is no longer simply the abstract fear of being out of work, but the *experience* of unemployment which secures the workers' cooperation; and we would assume that the sort of cooperation they will extend will be more to the employers' liking. In this case the employers are no longer dealing with incumbent workers who *may* be more or less intimidated by the threat of the sack, but with workers who will cooperate because they believe this is the only sort of work they can hope for. Rising productivity now requires unemployment not simply to discipline employees but to provide a pool of recruits.

The (official) Labour Force Survey seems to suggest that only a minority of temporary workers are recruited amongst the unemployed although the proportion of temporaries recruited amongst the unemployed might be rising (Meager 1986: 15). I believe that the proportion *is* increasing and also that the vast majority of casual and off-the-books workers who are not doing second jobs are already recruited amongst the unemployed. The most reliable evidence for this conclusion would be a 'cohort' study which investigated the experience of a group of workers over a period of time. However, such studies are usually thought to be too expensive and are therefore rare. One of the few recent British cohort studies was the national study of unemployed men, but unfortunately the sample for this cohort was drawn in 1978, that is *before* the use of new employment practices became common. Nevertheless, even this study suggested that one in four unemployed men had the sort of work histories which would be produced by spells of temporary or casual work (Moylan, 1984: 43-46)[7]. Evidence from the earlier chapters of this book would seem to indicate that this proportion has increased in recent years, and that employers are now recruiting workers who have been disciplined by their own immediate experience of unemployment.

While Chapter Six suggested that participation in contracting work *caused* downward social mobility, falling incomes and unemployment amongst contracting workers, the reverse is also true. The contracting workers were willing to put up with contracting work because they could no longer find the kind of jobs they used to do. The unemployed *in general* had shifted down the occupational hierarchy into occupations where they were ever more vulnerable to further unemployment, but this was *especially* true of contracting workers (no matter whether they were in or out of work at the time of the Port Talbot Survey). They could no longer find secure work in occupations they had been trained for and ended up trying to find work with contractors. It was therefore their own experience of unemployment that led them to accept contracting work (if they could find it).

We have now come some way from the simple (carrot and stick)

argument with which we began this section, but we are still some
way off a theory of the new employment practices. In large part, the
difficulty lies in the *generality* of the discussion so far. Employers
can use both the *fear* of unemployment amongst their existing
employees, and the *experience* of unemployment amongst recruits
drawn from the ranks of the unemployed, to secure workers'
cooperation in achieving any number of goals, not simply the
introduction of new employment practices[8]. Neither argument
captures what is unique about these practices.

The unique feature which all the new employment practices share
is that they do not lead to *permanent* employment. Because both the
simple argument (employees' fear of unemployment) and the idea
that employers recruit amongst the unemployed (experience of
unemployment) can be applied in cases where we are only
concerned with permanent jobs, neither gets to the heart of the
matter. To do this we must adopt the viewpoint of the employer.

Imagine that an employer wishes to improve the productivity of
the existing workforce, for whom the fear of unemployment seems
to have little impact. The employer decides to swap his workforce
for the one outside the factory gates, the unemployed who have
direct experience rather than abstract fear to spur their efforts to
improve productivity. But once inside the gates the unemployed
become the employed. The salutary effects of being out of work
begin to wear off, and their enthusiasm for increased productivity is
diminished accordingly. The faces of the workers have changed but
the problem remains: how can employers take full advantage of
rising unemployment, how can they make unemployment work for
them? The answer lies, of course, in the new employment practices.

Let us now adopt the viewpoint of the workers. When
unemployed workers are recruited as temporaries, casuals or off-
the-books workers the salutary effects of the experience of
unemployment take much longer to wear off (if ever) because these
workers *know* they are going to be unemployed again. They do not
simply have the *experience* of unemployment to discipline them but
the *expectation* of being unemployed again in a short time. It is
difficult or impossible for such workers to raise their expectations of
the rewards which go with *employment*, during the periods for
which they are in work, because they know this is a temporary
situation. This requires some explanation.

Because they know they will, or may (see below), be unemployed
tomorrow, it is as if these workers are re-engaged each morning
they come to work (this is literally true for casual workers of
course). Each morning they face the same choice as when they were
first hired: to take the job (on the employer's terms) or to stay out of
work. There is therefore no more possibility of considering pressing

the employer for improvements in the job on each successive day than there was on the day the worker was recruited. The risk of failure is too great. There is certainly no hope of success since these workers can be replaced as easily and as speedily as they were hired. For their temerity they may escape the sack on this occasion but may be sure they will not be re-hired when they are looking for work again.

Members of the workforce created by the new employment practices feel unable to press for improvements in pay or conditions, or even to resist further reductions in pay and deterioration in conditions, because they know they are going to be unemployed, and desperate for work, again. They have to bear in mind the difficulties of finding another job even when they are employed. They are *always* looking for work, and *always* act as if they are outside the factory gates, hammering to get in, even when they have employment.

For example, although the workers with experience of BSC contractors in the Port Talbot survey were often in work and were rarely out of work for a very long period of time[9], they thought in the same way as the long-term unemployed. Look at their responses to the attitude questions in the survey: they were more likely than the rest of the sample to say that rising unemployemnt was the change which had had the biggest personal impact on them, and they were more likely to agree that the unemployed should get more in state benefit. They were generally pessimistic about the future and more likely than the rest of the sample to *disagree* with the statement 'in my line of work I can always find another job'. These are not the attitudes of a group of men who have experienced unemployment but are now in permanent jobs. The contracting workers felt they were unemployed even when in work, and acted accordingly. In fact, even where they had been in work *for some time*, many contracting workers still behaved as if they were unemployed.

Temporary workers will behave as if they are unemployed even if their spells of employment turn out to be relatively long, *as long as* they do not *know* how long they will be in work. In Port Talbot, for example, uncertainty was part of the everyday lives of the irregular army of contracting workers. In many ways they were in a worse position than if they had been periodically engaged on *fixed-term* contracts which, if shorter than a spell with a contractor, at least put limits on the uncertain future. Chapter Five showed how contracting workers had to rely on hints from the foreman or their own powers of observation and guesswork in order to estimate how long they would be in work. This uncertainty made them feel like the unemployed: even if they had been in work for many months the job might still end tomorrow.

So far we have concluded that the new employment practices solve the (employers') problem of how to keep the salutary effects of unemployment from wearing off where workers are recruited amongst the unemployed. These effects do not wear off because the workforce required by the new employment practices is in a continuous state of 'job search'. Members of this workforce are always looking for work and the salutary effects of being out of work are always with them. But this formula does not exhaust the advantages of the new employment practices for the employers. Once the workforce has become accustomed to these practices the employers may also benefit at the recruitment stage.

It is likely that the workers who have become 'accustomed' to spells of insecure work interspersed with unemployment have lower expectations when they are *hired* for a job than workers who have had an uninterrupted spell, perhaps even a *long* uninterrupted spell, of unemployment. Participation in temporary, casual or off-the-books work lowers expectations when workers are out of work, as well as when they are in work. Such workers are not prepared to turn down any job offer, however lowly, in the hope that a better job may turn up soon. There are several reasons for this.

In the first place, workers with experience of temporary, casual or off-the-books work may actually have less chance of a good job than the long-term unemployed. For example, employers generally prefer to recruit workers who have stable career histories when they want to fill *permanent* posts, and may discriminate against applicants who have experience of temporary work. Once an individual has worked in a temporary job, his or her chances of finding permanent employment are reduced and she or he is forced to take more temporary work. There is little an individual worker can do to resist being drawn into this process.

Secondly, it may be that workers with experience of the new employment practices have a different assessment of prevailing labour market conditions from those who have simply been unemployed. Even if they believe their chance of a good job is no worse than the chance of other unemployed workers, they know from their experience of the labour market that this chance is very slim indeed. Some of the long-term unemployed, on the other hand, may still hope to find a good job, perhaps one as good as the job they lost months ago. They therefore only apply for comparable jobs and do not realise that workers with similar qualifications and experience have been forced down the market and are taking jobs which they would once have rejected[10].

Finally, workers with experience of temporary, casual or off-the-books work know that *their* job search does not end when they make a successful application for employment. Since they will be making job applications for the foreseeable future (each time they become unemployed again) they cannot afford higher standards which would lead them to refuse an offer of work, however unattractive, because such a refusal would damage their *future* chances. Thus in Chapter Five we saw how Frank Clark's concern for his reputation amongst the contracting employers meant that he was reluctant to be seen to turn down any sort of work, no matter if it was for one shift or off-the-books.

To summarise, the new employment practices do not merely arrest the process whereby the salutary effects of unemployment gradually wear off once an unemployed worker finds a job. They also make these salutary effects still more vivid. Workers with experience of the new employment practices, like the contracting workers in the household survey, therefore accept jobs which even the long-term unemployed might reject.

An employer who uses the new employment practices reaps many benefits. Such employers can shape conditions of employment as they wish. Chapter Five showed how such employers can find workers who are prepared to work for a shift at a time (and to work long hours without notice) on-or off-the-books. Chapter Five also showed that, even when they are in 'proper' temporary employment, such workers can be paid low wages with few or no fringe benefits. Employers can demand hard work for these meagre returns, and win increases in productivity as a result.

We can now see a third, and final, aspect of the relationship between rising unemployment and productivity. Increases in productivity do not merely require unemployment because this produces *fear* amongst employees or because this provides a pool of new recruits who have been disciplined by the *experience* of unemployment. Rather, unemployment is necessary to increased productivity because productivity will increase more quickly if workers are not simply recruited from amongst the unemployed, but returned to unemployment at regular intervals. Rising productivity depends on the workers' knowledge that they will become unemployed, and in search of work once more, in the near future. Nowhere is this more evident than in Port Talbot where unemployment — through the mechanism of casual or temporary work with contractors — is now one of the conditions necessary to the production of steel.

It is also now evident that *illegal* casual work is not some temporary aberration but the employers' logical best buy amongst the new employment practices. With off-the-books casual work they can literally *bring the unemployed into the workplace* and solve for ever the problem of what becomes of the unemployed once they are inside the factory gates. But employers are not always able to use illegal casual workers and so they use temporary workers (preferably *not* on fixed-term contracts) instead. This serves the same purpose since these temporary workers soon think, and act, like the unemployed only more so. Employers solve the problem of how to make *unemployment* work for them by making the *unemployed* work for them. All of the new employment practices serve to weaken, and on occasion destroy, the distinction between employment and unemployment[11].

If the new employment practices destroy the distinction between *being* employed and *being* unemployed we would expect that they also serve to blur the distinction between the employed and the unemployed. This is, of course, exactly what has happened: because the distinction has been blurred we have to turn to terms like 'under-employment' or 'sub-employment' which are meant to imply a *combination* of employment and unemployment. In Chapter Six we learnt that half of the sample of Port Talbot men who were currently unemployed (and available for work) had contracting experience. If the same sample had been drawn a few months later, roughly the same proportion would have been out of work but many of the names of the unemployed men would have changed. Because a survey (unlike a cohort study — see above) is a snapshot it gives the impression that there is a division between employed and unemployed when none exists in fact.

It is now clear that our theory about the relationship between the new employment practices and unemployment fits the facts about the Port Talbot labour market more closely than any theory which sees unemployment as a scrap heap. The extent of contracting experience in the sample of Port Talbot men goes a long way towards explaining why there was no hard-and-fast dividing line between the employed and the unemployed. The contracting workers occupied some sort of limbo between the two: a curious kind of unemployment which Chapter One described as 'under-employment'. They were not long-term unemployed but did not have secure jobs and were continually changing from one status to the other.

The employers who use new employment practices are effecting important changes in the labour market. However unplanned employers' use of the new employment practices might be (see above), it would be a mistake to conclude that they are merely responding to conditions which they had no hand in creating. Meager, for example, suggests that employers' employment strategies are determined by changes in the labour market over which they have no control (1986: 14), yet their strategies are eroding the distinction between the employed and the unemployed.

Once insecure jobs have been created (and filled) by one employer the snowball begins to roll and many more workers are drawn into insecure employment. Workers from a variety of occupations are drawn into the market for temporary work and employers are able to recruit them into an increasing number of jobs which were once held by permanent employees.

This does not, of course, mean that employers change labour market conditions *intentionally*. However, when the employer is as large as BSC there must be some suspicion that the erosion of the distinction between the employed and unemployed was a conscious goal. BSC was once known as the epitome of a stable employer. Treasure Island and its counterparts in other steel towns appeared to offer life-time employment. But BSC made half of its workforce at Port Talbot unemployed and then brought the unemployed into the workplace[12] as contracting workers.

**Footnotes**
1. Or because (contracting) firms were not *classified* as part of the steel industry (see also Leadbeater and Lloyd, 1987: 25, 141). Either explanation may account, in part, for the fact that numbers of male temporaries did not incease between 1983 and 1985 (*Social Trends*, 1987).
2. Although note that BSC did use significant numbers of temporary workers at some of its plants. For example, at Hartlepool BSC used a 'call list' of ex-BSC employees who were employed (directly) on short-term contracts. A small core workforce was maintained with the extra workers being drafted in only for large orders (*Guardian*, 15 January 1983).
3. Agriculture, construction, distribution, hotel and catering, and other services. The Department of Employment recognised the growth in importance of the self-employed when they decided to accept self-employed vacancies in 1981:
   'These vacancies ... reflect the change towards contracting out work that would previously have been carried out by employees.'
   (*Employment Gazette*, October 1985).
4. With the possible exception of John Atkinson's theory of the 'flexible firm'. Atkinson's theory recalls both the work of Andrew Friedman (1978), and general work on 'dual' or 'segmented' labour markets, so far as he argues that employers distinguish between 'core' and 'peripheral' workers. The workers involved in new employment practices can only be described as 'peripheral' if a 'core' workforce exists alongside them (see footnote [2] above). There is some evidence that employers no longer feel so much in need of a core of stable employees, especially employees who may think they have secure *tenure* of their jobs. Thus a source close to BSC's Chief Executive distinguished the 'core-periphery' practices of BSC from those used by competitors in Japan. He told me that BSC could not go as far as the Japanese because British employers were not 'paternalistic like the Japanese'.
5. Readers may note, however, that some of what follows also applies to the practices of other Port Talbot employers, especially the defunct computer manufacturer, 'Griffin', described in Chapter Three.
6. This allows us to add another conclusion to the discussion of 'real' jobs in Chapter Eight. There it was suggested that, in some areas, the substitution of 'real' for 'artificial' jobs created unemployment. While this remains true, it is

also true that, *in some areas, creating unemployment was necessary to the creation of real jobs.* Note that it is still necessary to include the qualification, 'in some areas'. The carrot may still be popular in some parts of Britain, especially the South East of England, where workers are offered a share of increased productivity. The stick is more commonly used in areas like South Wales (where workers are threatened with the sack unless they produce more). Here the employers' usual strategy is to make some of the workforce 'redundant' and then expect the remainder to produce the same (or more) output in the knowledge that their fear of unemployment will guarantee their compliance.

7. See Pond (1980) for a summary of related evidence from the early 1970s.

8. In the United States, for example, employers are making use of recruits drawn from the ranks of the unemployed in order to introduce dual wage structures which pay one rate to existing employees and a lower rate to the new recruits (*New Society*, 26 January 1984).

9. The fact that contracting workers were more likely to receive the higher rate of welfare benefit (unemployment benefit) proves that their periods of unemployment were shorter (see Chapter Six).

10. In the economists' partisan language, the 'reservation wage' of the long- term unemployed is 'unrealistic'.

11. If the 'new' employment practices turn out to be not new, but a revival, then the same applies to this contribution to our understanding of these practices. Firstly, something close to this formulation was implicit in Marx's description of the 'reserve army of labour':

> 'The third category of the relative surplus population, the stagnant, forms a part of the active labour army, but with *extremely irregular employment.* Hence it furnishes to capital an inexhaustible reservoir of disposable labour power. Its conditions of life sink below the average normal level of the working-class; this makes it at once the broad basis of special branches of capitalist exploitation. It is characterised by maximum working-time, and minimum of wages.'

> (*Marx 1974: 602, emphasis added*)

12. That so many of them were BSC's own former workers was particularly useful since no extra training was required. Note that employers which, *unlike* BSC, intend to use temporaries, casuals or off-the-books workers for *additional* recruitment will not affect the labour market in quite the same way since there will be no *immediate* rise in unemployment.

# BIBLIOGRAPHY

Atkinson J. 1984 *Emerging UK Work Patterns*, Brighton: Institute for Manpower Studies.

Aylen J. 1982 'Plant size and efficiency in the steel industry, an international comparison', *National Institute Economic Review*, 100, May.

Aylen J. 1983 'Are we doing enough?', *Iron and Steel International*, August.

Bresnen M.K. *et al* 1985 'The flexibility of recruitment in the construction industry: formalisation or re-casualisation?', *Sociology*, vol 19, no 1, pp 108-124.

British Steel Corporation 1979 *The Return to Financial Viability: a Business Proposal for 1980-81*, London: BSC.

British Steel Corporation 1979a *Changing your Job*, first edition, London: BSC.

British Steel Corporation 1980 *The Return to Financial Viability: Presentation of South Wales Options*, London: BSC.

Bromley R. and Gerry C. 1979 'Who are the casual poor?' in R. Bromley and C. Gerry (eds) *Casual Work and Poverty in Third World Cities*, Chichester: John Wiley.

Brown R. 1983 'Work: past, present and future' in K. Thompson (ed) *Work, Employment and Unemployment*, London: Open University.

Bryer R.A., Brignall T.J. and Maunders A.R. 1982 *Accounting for British Steel*, Aldershot: Gower.

Cottrell E. 1981 *The Giant with Feet of Clay: the British Steel Industry 1945-81*, London: Centre for Policy Studies.

CIS (Counter Information Services) 1982 *Private Line — the Future of British Telecom*, CIS Report no 32, London: CIS.

Danson M. 1982 'The industrial structure and labour market segmentation: urban and regional implications', *Regional Studies*, vol 16, no 4, pp 255-265.

Ferman L.A. 1978 *Analysis of the Irregular Economy: Cash Flow in the Informal Sector*, Report to the Bureau of Employment and Training, Michigan: Department of Labor.

Fevre R. 1981 *The Labour Process in Bradford*, Bradford: EEC/DES Transition to Work Project, Bradford College.

Fevre R. 1984 *Cheap Labour and Racial Discrimination*, Aldershot: Gower.

Fevre R. 1984a *Employment and Unemployment in Port Talbot: a reference paper*, School of Social Studies Occasional Paper No 6, Swansea: University College.

Fevre R. 1984b *A Postal Survey of Employment in Port Talbot*, School of Social Studies Occasional Paper No 7, Swansea: University College.

Fevre R. 1986 'Contract work in the recession' in K. Purcell *et al* (eds) *The Changing Experience of Employment*, London: Macmillan.

Fevre R. 1986a 'Redundancy and the labour market: the role of "readaption benefits"' in R.M. Lee (ed) *Redundancy Lay-offs and Plant Closures: the Social Impact*, London: Croom Helm.

Friedman A. 1978 *Industry and Labour*, London: Macmillan.

Fryer R. 1981 'State, redundancy and the law' in R. Fryer *et al* (eds) *Law State and Society*, London: Croom Helm.

Gerry C. 1983 *Recession, Restructuring and the Rediscovery of a 'Black' Economy*, Paper to Annual Conference of British Sociological Association, Cardiff.

Glamorgan Education Authority 1950-1970 *Reports on the Youth Employment Service*, Cardiff: Education Department, County Hall.

Le Grand J. and Robinson R. (eds) 1984 *Privatisation and the Welfare State*, London, Allen and Unwin.

De Grazia R. 1984 *Clandestine Employment*, Geneva: International Labour Organisation.

Harrigan K.R. 1985 *Strategic Flexibility: a management guide to changing times*, Lexington, Mass.,: D.C. Heath.

Harris C.C. and the Swansea Redundancy Group (forthcoming) *Redundancy and Recession in South Wales*, Oxford: Blackwell.

Hicks C.A. 1980 'The use of contractors for maintenance: benefits and pitfalls' in *Minimizing the Cost of Maintenance*, London: Metals Society.

House of Commons Committee on Welsh Affairs 1980 *Minutes of Evidence, Session 1979-1980*, London: HMSO.

House of Commons Committee on Trade and Industry 1983 *Minutes of Evidence, Session 1982-1983*, London: HMSO.

Howe L. 1985 *Unemployment: Historical Aspects of Data Collection and the Black Economy in Belfast*, Paper to Conference of Anthropological Studies Association.

Iron and Steel Trades Confederation 1980 *New Deal for Steel*, London: ISTC.

Leadbeater C. and Lloyd J. 1987 *In Search of Work*, Harmondsworth: Penguin.

Marx K. 1974 *Capital*, Volume One, London: Lawrence and Wishart.

Mattera P. 1985 *Off The Books*, London: Pluto.

Meager N. 1986 'Temporary work in Britain' *Employment Gazette*, January, pp 7-15.

Moore R. 1981 'Aspects of segmentation in the UK building industry labour market' in F. Wilkinson (ed) *The Dynamics of Labour Market Segmentation*, London: Academic Press.

Morgan K. 1983 'Restructuring steel: the crises of labour and locality in Britain', *International Journal of Urban and Regional Research*, Vol 7, No 2, pp 175-201.

Moylan S. *et al* 1984 *For Richer or Poorer*, DHSS Cohort Study of Unemployed Men, Research Report No 11, London: HMSO.

National Joint Council for the Engineering Construction Industry 1983 *National Agreement for the Engineering Construction Industry*, London: NJCECI.

Norris G.M. 1978 'Unemployment, subemployment and personal characteristics', *Sociological Review*, Vol 26, Nos 1 and 2.

Pollert A. 1988 'Dismantling "Flexibility"' *Capital and Class*, No 34.

Pond C. 1980 'The structure of unemployment in Britain' *International Journal of Social Economics*, Vol 7 No 7, pp 353-365.

Scase R. and Goffee R. 1982 *The Entrepreneurial Middle Class*, London: Croom Helm.

Upham M. 1980 'The BSC: retrospect and prospect' *Industrial Relations Journal*, July/August.

Wales TUC 1976 *Annual Report*

Walker J. and Moore R. 1983 *Privatisation of Local Government Services*, London: Workers' Educational Association.

Williams K. *et al* 1983 *Why are the British bad at Manufacturing?*, London: Routledge.

Worsley P. 1976 'Proletarians, subproletarians, lumpen proletarians, marginalidados, migrants, urban peasants and urban poor' *Sociology*, Vol 10 No 1.

# Index

50, 98-9, 104, 106, 148, 156n
transport 54, 56, 59, 61, 63, 65, 66, 69, 74, 132

UCATT 91
USA 156n
under-employment 15, 154
'unemployables' 99, 107
unemployment:
 benefit 11, 87, 89, 95, 105, 106, 156n
 and employment 15-16, 50-1, 53, 82-92, 106-7, 147-55, 156n
 expectations of 148-54
 long-term 15, 98, 148, 152, 154
 official figures 41, 49-51, 52n, 109n
 and recruitment 43, 50-1, 107, 148-54
 and social class 98-9, 107n
 and technical change 138
 women 49, 50
 youth 50, 52n
 *see also* BSC workers, contracting workers, Port Talbot, productivity,

redundancies, temporary work, West Glamorgan
University College of Swansea 68, 97, 107n
Upham, M. 16n, 110, 135
Urban Aid 47

WDA 43, 45-7
Walker, J. and Moore, R. 16n
welders 13, 65, 67, 82
Welsh Office 47
West Glamorgan:
 employment 24-5, 49;
 redundancies 38-9;
 unemployment 41
Williams, K. *et al* 140n
'withdrawal' from labour market 98, 106;
 and redundancies 50
Work Measurement Incentive Scheme 26